THE
Marriage
& Family
PRESENTATION GUIDE

THE
Marriage & Family
PRESENTATION GUIDE

Laurie Cope Grand

John Wiley & Sons, Inc.
New York • Chichester • Weinheim • Brisbane • Singapore • Toronto

ISBN 0-471-37444-X

Printed in the United States of America.

10 9 8 7 6 5 4 3 2 1

Contents

Acknowledgments ix

Introduction xi

Chapter 1. How to Build Your Practice with Presentations 1.1

    Exhibit 1.1   A Sample Brochure 1.4
    Exhibit 1.2   A Sample Press Release 1.6
    Exhibit 1.3   A Sample Workshop Evaluation Form 1.7

Chapter 2. Presentation Pointers 2.1

    Exhibit 2.1   Types of Seating Arrangements 2.7

Chapter 3. 12 Tips for Marketing Your Practice 3.1

Chapter 4. Before the Wedding: Skills for Marriage Success 4.1

    Exhibit 4.1   Presentation Outline 4.4
    Exhibit 4.2   Presentation Script 4.5
    Handout 4.1   The Nine Tasks of a Successful Marriage .4.18
    Handout 4.2   Why Marriages Succeed or Fail 4.20
    Handout 4.3   Four Skills to Build Your Marriage 4.21
    Handout 4.4   Four Marriage Destroyers 4.22
    Handout 4.5   What Do You Value? 4.23
    Handout 4.6   My Expectations 4.25
    Handout 4.7   Whose Responsibility Is It? 4.28
    Handout 4.8   What's Next? 4.29

Contents

Chapter 5.   The Good Marriage: Skills for Making Your Marriage Thrive .5.1

Exhibit 5.1	Presentation Outline	5.5
Exhibit 5.2	Presentation Script	5.6
Handout 5.1	12 Roadblocks to Effective Communication	5.16
Handout 5.2	Active Listening Practice Exercises	5.17
Handout 5.3	Listening Skills	5.18
Handout 5.4	Assertive Communication	5.20
Handout 5.5	You-Messages, I-Messages	5.22
Handout 5.6	Managing Conflict	5.24
Handout 5.7	A Better Response	5.25
Handout 5.8	Five Ways to Interrupt Anger	5.27
Handout 5.9	Business Skills/Marriage Skills	5.28
Handout 5.10	What's Next?	5.30

Chapter 6.   The Marriage Checkup .6.1

Exhibit 6.1	Presentation Outline	6.5
Exhibit 6.2	Presentation Script	6.6
Handout 6.1	The Marriage Checkup	6.8

Chapter 7.   Recovering from Infidelity .7.1

Exhibit 7.1	Presentation Outline	7.4
Exhibit 7.2	Presentation Script	7.5
Handout 7.1	Reasons for Infidelity	7.12
Handout 7.2	Signs of Infidelity	7.13
Handout 7.3	Infidelity Facts	7.14
Handout 7.4	Infidelity: The Emotional Impact and Other Consequences	7.15
Handout 7.5	How to Recover from Infidelity	7.16
Handout 7.6	How to Prevent Infidelity	7.17

Chapter 8.   Single-Parent Survival Skills .8.1

Exhibit 8.1	Presentation Outline	8.5
Exhibit 8.2	Presentation Script	8.6
Handout 8.1	10 Ways to Speed Your Recovery Process	8.12
Handout 8.2	Listening Skills	8.14
Handout 8.3	28 Single-Parent Survival Strategies	8.16

Chapter 9.   Minimizing the Emotional Toll of Divorce 9.1

Exhibit 9.1	Presentation Outline	9.4
Exhibit 9.2	Presentation Script	9.5
Handout 9.1	Children's Divorce Rights	9.10
Handout 9.2	36 Divorce Survival Strategies	9.11

Contents

Chapter 10. Avoiding Emotional Disasters: Just for Teens 10.1

Exhibit 10.1   Presentation Outline 10.4
Exhibit 10.2   Presentation Script 10.5
Handout 10.1 12 Survival Strategies for Teens 10.13
Handout 10.2 Who Am I? 10.15
Handout 10.3 Assertive Behavior 10.17
Handout 10.4 Your Opinion Counts 10.19
Handout 10.5 Managing Your Emotions 10.20

Chapter 11. Managing Conflict Creatively 11.1

Exhibit 11.1   Presentation Outline 11.4
Exhibit 11.2   Presentation Script 11.5
Handout 11.1 Handling Conflicts 11.12
Handout 11.2 Active Listening 11.13
Handout 11.3 Assertive Communication Skills 11.14
Handout 11.4 Conflict Deescalation 11.15
Handout 11.5 Preventing Conflict 11.16

Chapter 12. Managing the Emotional Challenges of Caregiving   **12.1**

Exhibit 12.1   Presentation Outline 12.5
Exhibit 12.2   Presentation Script 12.6
Handout 12.1 Facts about Caregiving 12.13
Handout 12.2 The Five Stages of Grief Recovery 12.14
Handout 12.3 Sources of Stress 12.15
Handout 12.4 Signs That a Caregiver Needs Help 12.17
Handout 12.5 Caregiver Survival Tips 12.18
Handout 12.6 Caregiver Bill of Rights 12.19

Chapter 13. Parenting Your Teenager 13.1

Exhibit 13.1   Presentation Outline 13.4
Exhibit 13.2   Presentation Script 13.5
Handout 13.1 Stages of Development 13.14
Handout 13.2 How to Maintain Communication with Your Teen 13.15
Handout 13.3 Preventing High-Risk Behavior 13.16
Handout 13.4 Characteristics of Effective Families 13.17
Handout 13.5 Drugs and Alcohol 13.18
Handout 13.6 Sexuality 13.19
Handout 13.7 Depression 13.20
Handout 13.8 Eating Disorders 13.21
Handout 13.9 How to Build Your Teen's Self-Esteem 13.22

About the Disk D.1

Acknowledgments

I want to thank the following people who influenced this project in various ways. First, my thanks and deep appreciation to Kelly Franklin, Publisher at John Wiley & Sons. I am also grateful to Susan Back, LCSW, my dear sister and friend, who encouraged me to share my ideas for presentations with other therapists. I also appreciate the guidance, influence, and support of my mentors and dear friends Dr. Jules Burg, Rachel Bar, Anne LeMay, and Kristie Carmody, who taught me much of what I know about being a therapist. And I dedicate this project to Renée Lang Burg, who left this world too early but whose influence will always be felt. Finally, thanks for the support and love of my dear husband Mark, my strong and capable daughter Lisa, and my mother (who told me I could do anything), Jean Hamilton Cope.

Introduction

What This Book Includes

The Marriage and Family Presentation Guide includes 10 presentations for you to use to market your counseling practice. Each title includes a detailed presenter's outline, a list of reading material for your reference when you are preparing for a presentation, a sample marketing letter, and a press release.

Customize to Meet Your Audience's Needs

You may wish to mix and match the content of the presentation outlines and the handouts to meet the specific needs of various audiences. You may also want to change the name of your presentations to more exactly fit the needs and interests of your audiences. For example, "The Marriage Checkup" could be recast as "Get Your Marriage Ready for Retirement" when it is presented to a group of older adults. "The Good Marriage: Skills for Making Your Marriage Thrive" could become "How to Build a Successful Long-Term Relationship" or "Make Your Relationship Last Forever" when presented to almost any group of adults.

Participant Handouts

Each topic includes a set of participant handouts. You may remove them from this book and reproduce them or use the files on the enclosed disk to edit and print them. Be creative: Mix and match the topics and alter the handouts to fit your personality and to meet the needs of your audience.

Visual Aids

Visuals always add value to a presentation. I recommend that you purchase a blank flip-chart pad and some markers from an office supply store and prepare posters before your presentation.

Videos

Most of the presentations include references to short scenes from popular movies that many of your participants may have seen. Including these videos as examples of various points in your presentations is a way to make them more interesting. If you can think of other scenes to add or use instead of the examples provided, feel free to substitute them.

Some videos may require that you obtain the permission of the copyright holder before you use them in certain types of presentations. Find out what the requirements are and obtain the necessary permission.

Be sure to check with the facility where you are giving your presentation to be sure they have a working VCR (in VHS format) and monitor. If they don't, consider bringing your own equipment.

THE
Marriage
& Family
PRESENTATION GUIDE

Chapter 1

How to Build
Your Practice
with Presentations

Research Your Audience

First, *decide whom you want to market your services to.* The 10 workshops in this collection contain information relevant to just about everyone who is in a family or personal relationship. Any organized group has people who need to know how to manage conflict and build strong relationships. Schools and religious groups attract teens and their parents, as well as single parents and people recovering from infidelity and divorce.

There are many places to *look for names and addresses of organizations* to offer your services to. Look through the Yellow Pages and the Chamber of Commerce Community Guide. The Chamber may publish annual listings of groups that may even include names of people to contact. You may be able to purchase mailing labels or obtain lists on disk, making it easy to develop a targeted mailing list.

Search the Internet for names and addresses of contacts. Many cities and towns publish lists of local groups and organizations on their web sites. If you don't know where to begin, go to a search engine like Yahoo! or Lycos (www.yahoo.com or www.lycos.com) and type in the name of your city or town.

Design a brochure. Please see the sample brochure, Exhibit 1.1. It was designed with Microsoft Publisher 2000 and may be printed on paper purchased from an office supply store or from a company such as PaperDirect. They offer hundreds of beautiful styles. Call 1-800-A-PAPERS or visit www.paperdirect .com to request a catalog.

In your brochure, describe the series of workshops and offer to present them as a *community service.* Send the brochure to every potential organization in your area. Follow up with a phone call.

Another option is to *design a separate flyer* for each of the workshops in your series. Send them one at a time, once every six or eight weeks, to local groups. Send them to every kind of group in your area— schools, churches, synagogues, clubs, clinics, hospitals, doctors' offices. They all know people who need the skills addressed in these workshops.

Design a workbook based on the handouts. Send them to local groups along with a brochure or flyer offering your services as a presenter.

Offer to speak on a local *radio or television show* about any of the topics. Put together a media kit with your glossy photo and bio, along with an outline of what you'd like to talk about.

Send your brochure and a letter to the managers of local bookstores. Offer to *conduct free workshops* during the spring or fall months at the bookstores or at your office. In your letter, request a meeting with each store manager. At the meeting, discuss your plan. Offer to supply the brochures or flyers and request that they be stacked at the wrap desk or by the front door. Visit the stores regularly to make sure there is a supply of the flyers available for customers to take.

If you are planning to offer your workshops for free, you may want to consider *asking the company to pay for the cost of copying* and packaging your handouts.

Offer to *conduct the "Single Parent Survival Skills" workshop* at the local pediatrician's office. Send a cover letter and flyer or brochure to every pediatrician in your area and follow up with a phone call.

Think about other logical places to offer the workshops on marriage-related topics. Here are a few ideas: churches and synagogues, parent organizations at public and private schools, and groups such as Business and Professional Women.

Consider working with a partner, especially if you are anxious about speaking before groups. Having another therapist as a partner to co-lead your workshops with you will most likely considerably lessen your anxiety level. He or she can also help you brainstorm ways to market the workshops and participate in developing, distributing, and *paying for* the marketing materials.

Maximize your impact with *good timing* by anticipating when people are likely to be interested in certain topics. For example, you might send a flyer to your local bridal store in February offering to present a "Before the Wedding" workshop in the spring. "The Marriage Checkup" is a perfect topic for an adult education group at the local church or synagogue just before Valentine's Day.

When an organization asks you to present your workshop on site, ask to *meet with a few of the officers* to discuss their needs. Prepare a list of questions to ask before you go. Find out which workshops they are interested in and why. Ask them what their goals are and how your workshops might help accomplish them.

Find out if the group has a *member newsletter.* If they do, offer to write a short article that's related to your workshop. You are free to use the text of your outlines and handouts, as long as you give credit to the original sources.

Use the information in the outlines to *write a series of articles* for your local newspaper.

Advertise. Arrange to present the workshops and run ads in your local paper. Include your picture in the ad and a reference to your upcoming workshop.

Write a *press release* about your event and send it with your glossy publicity photo to every local media outlet. Make sure you have the permission of your contact at the organization where you are making your presentation. There is a sample (see Exhibit 1.2), and each presentation outline has wording for a press release.

Package your handouts to look professional and impressive. You want people to say "wow!" when they see them. Spend the money to package them in a nice folder and place your business card in each one. Avery makes a nice folder—you can print your own design on the cover, using your own printer. They are somewhat expensive, but remember that you want to make a strong impression.

Following Up Your Presentation

Prepare an *evaluation form* for participants to complete after your presentation. It can be as simple as Exhibit 1.3. Ask people to complete it and leave it by the door as they leave. It will provide you with useful feedback for next time. If the feedback is favorable, you can use it to market future presentations. If it's not so favorable, just learn from it. There will always be people who like you and people who don't.

The day after your workshop, send a hand-written *thank you note* to your contact at the organization or group.

Exhibit 1.1   A Sample Brochure

How to Recover From Infidelity

Infidelity is more common than most people realize. It is estimated that 60% of men and 40% of women today will have an extramarital affair during their marriage. This workshop explores the forces that lead to infidelity and what must happen for couples to heal.

- What infidelity is
- Statistics and current research
- Key issues: the emotional impact
- How people recover from infidelity
- How to avoid becoming an infidelity statistic

Place your photo here

Community Service Workshops

Would the members of your community or religious group value a presentation on one of these topics? Please call *Your Name* to schedule your workshop.

Workshops for churches and synagogues may be copresented with one of your group's leaders (pastor, rabbi, congregation leader, etc.).

All workshops are offered at no charge as a community service.

Presented by
Your Name
Your License
(555) 555-1234
www.yourwebsite.com

Good Marriage
Workshops

Help your group members build strong relationships with these community service workshops:

- Before the Wedding: Skills for Marriage Success
- Lessons from Current Research: How to Build a Good Marriage
- Keep Your Marriage Healthy with the Marriage Checkup
- Recovering from Infidelity

Presented by
Your Name
Your License
(555) 555-1234
www.yourwebsite.com

Before the Wedding: Skills for Marriage Success

This workshop is designed for couples who have decided to get married. It presents current research on marriage and outlines the skills needed for success.

- Marriage success: What the research says
- Expectations, needs and goals
- Four marriage-building skills
- Nine marriage tasks
- Four marriage-destroying behaviors

You may wish to combine or modify the content from these workshops to suit the needs of your group.

Lessons from Current Research: How to Build a Good Marriage

This workshop is designed for couples who have been married for a year or longer. Its premise is that successful relationships require a set of specific skills that can be learned and practiced.

- How to manage your marriage like a business—planning, organizing, and setting goals
- Listening skills
- Assertive communication
- How to resolve conflicts
- Managing anger
- Giving and receiving constructive feedback

Developed by Your Name
Your License
(555) 555-1234
www.yourwebsite.com

Protect Your Marriage With an Annual Relationship Checkup

Most people have no trouble remembering to schedule an annual physical exam, and most of us visit the dentist every six months. Why should a relationship be any different? With worksheets and checklists, this workshop enables couples to focus on the following aspects of their relationship and evaluate its health:

- Communication
- Goals and objectives
- Managing conflict
- Family life
- Fun
- Money
- Sex
- Spiritual life

Exhibit 1.2   A Sample Press Release

For Immediate Release

Ann Carmody
5665 Alegria St.
Tarzana, CA 91827
555/555-1726

CONTACT: Ann Carmody

"Build a Good Marriage" Series
Presented by Marriage and Family Therapist

Tarzana, CA—January 13, 20XX—Ann Carmody, PhD, is presenting a series of workshops in the West San Fernando Valley. The series will meet on Tuesdays from 7 to 9 p.m. starting on February 1. All four sessions will be held at the Tarzana Counseling Center on Alegria Street. The sessions are limited to 20 participants and are being presented as a public service.

"Building a good marriage is a challenge for most people," says Dr. Carmody. "With the rate of divorce at 50 percent, few of us have good role models to learn the skills that make marriage last. What few people realize is that successful marriages are built on some very specific skills that almost anyone can learn." The series of four workshops includes "Before the Wedding: Skills for Marriage Success," "The Good Marriage: Skills for Making Your Marriage Thrive," "Marriage Checkup," and "Recovering from Infidelity." Dr. Carmody offers the workshops at the Tarzana Counseling Center as well as for community groups.

Dr. Carmody has been a licensed marriage and family therapist in California since 1985. To make a reservation or for more information, call the Tarzana Counseling Center at (555) 555-1726.

# # # #

Exhibit 1.3   A Sample Workshop Evaluation Form

Workshop Evaluation Form

Thank you for your comments about today's workshop. Please answer the following questions and leave this form at the door.

1. What did you like best about today's workshop?

2. What did you learn?

3. What did you like least?

4. What suggestions do you have for future workshops?

Thank you for your comments and suggestions.

Chapter 2

Presentation Pointers

Chapter 2

Many people are uncomfortable with the idea of speaking before a group. Here are some ways you can prepare yourself to give a professional, successful presentation.

1. *Learn about your audience and their needs.*

Who is your audience?

Ask your contact in the organization to describe who will be in the audience. Some questions to ask include:

- What are the audience members likely to know about you and your subject?
- How are they likely to feel about being there?
- What do they already know about your topic?
- What are their views about psychotherapy and psychotherapists?
- What special needs do they have?

What is the purpose of the meeting?

Some questions to ask about the meeting include:

- Why is this group meeting?
- What is the occasion? Is this a regular weekly or monthly meeting, and is a speaker usually invited?
- What kinds of speakers have made presentations in the past?

How formal is the occasion?

- Will this be a small group gathered around a table, or a large group (50 or more) sitting auditorium-style in rows of seats?
- How well do the participants know one another? Are they used to some kind of interaction and participation, or are they expecting a lecture?
- Will there be a lectern, microphone, and audiovisual equipment?
- If this is a small group, is there an easel and flip-chart pad available?

What is the context of your presentation?

- Are you the only speaker, perhaps the featured speaker at a luncheon meeting, or are you one of several?
- How does your topic relate to the other subjects being discussed before and after your presentation?

How long should you speak?

- Find out the total amount of time available.
- Will there be one or more breaks?
- Is time for questions and answers included?

At what time of day will you speak?

- If you are scheduled to speak during a meal, expect audience members to be distracted.
- If you are speaking after a meal, build some exercises and participation into your presentation to avoid having people drift off to sleep.

2. *Arrange the meeting room.*

Arrange the seating.
If at all possible, before your presentation, arrange the meeting room to enable people to see and hear you easily. (Refer to Exhibit 2.1.) Choose an arrangement that fits the purpose of the meeting. For example:

- Auditorium-style seating works best for large groups (more than 50) and lectures.

- Tables of 6 to 10 people are appropriate when participants will be writing and interacting with each other.

- Rows of chairs and tables with a center aisle enable people to take notes and allow the speaker to walk into the audience.

Will you use a lectern?
- A lectern can be comforting if you are nervous. It gives you something to hide behind and a place to put your notes.

- Standing next to the lectern or stepping away from it makes you more accessible to the audience.

- Unless you are speaking to a very small group, plan to stand during your presentation. Speaking while seated makes you appear much less powerful.

3. *Prepare appropriate visual aids.*

Prepare flip charts and posters.
It is always more interesting for the audience when you provide something for them to look at. Posters of your key points are a very effective way to add interest and clarity to your presentation.

- An inexpensive idea is to make posters of your key points on a newsprint flip-chart pad. Prepare this ahead of time and rehearse your presentation using the flip chart. Make sure the printing is large enough for people in the back of the room to see.

- Inexpensive pads may be purchased at an office supply store.

- Another advantage of having visuals prepared ahead of time is that it makes your key points easier to remember.

- You can rely on the information on your flip chart to guide you as you make your presentation.

- You can also write a few more key ideas lightly in pencil as reminders while you speak. Knowing this information is there for you helps reduce the jitters.

Prepare slides.
You may have slides made for a professional touch.

- Expect each slide to cost several dollars, and allow enough time to have them made.

- If you decide to use slides, practice using the equipment before the audience enters the room.

- If you plan to use the remote control, try it out before your presentation to be sure it works properly.

- Stay away from the screen as you are speaking, or you will block the audience's view. You will also be lit up along with the screen, and you may look a bit strange.

Prepare transparencies.

Transparencies are another inexpensive yet professional way to provide information visually.

- Place each transparency in a cardboard frame (which you can purchase inexpensively at an office supply store). Transparencies tend to stick together from static electricity, and the frame prevents this.

- Turn off the transparency machine when you switch to the next visual. Turn it back on when you've placed the next transparency on it. Leaving the machine on with no transparency can feel blinding to the audience.

- Stay away from the screen as you are speaking, or you will block the audience's view. You will also be lit up along with the screen, and you may look a bit strange.

4. *Prepare your presentation.*

Develop the outline and content.

- Your presentation should have a beginning, a middle, and an end.

- Include as many examples as you can think of—at least one for each point. Examples and illustrations bring your presentation to life and make it more interesting.

- Develop about 25 percent more content than you think you'll need. Then you won't have to worry about running out of things to say.

- If possible, make your presentation interactive. Build in a few exercises for people to do, either individually or in small groups.

- Prepare questions to ask the participants throughout your presentation. Note a few answers to each question, in case no one responds.

Design the handouts.

- Handouts should be written in simple language with plenty of white space.

- Include your name and phone number on your handouts.

- Always credit your sources.

- Prepare more handouts than you think you'll need.

Gather the supplies.

Pack the following supplies for your presentation:

- Your outline
- Participant handouts
- Markers

- Masking tape
- Business cards
- Your practice brochure
- Visual aids (slides, transparencies, or posters)

Optional supplies include:

- Videos (cued to the correct scene)
- Audiotapes or CDs
- Cassette or CD player

5. *Rehearse your presentation.*

Visit the meeting room.	If it's possible to visit the room where your presentation will be held, doing so will accomplish a number of things.

- You will feel more confident and calm before your meeting when you can visualize the setting. The unknown is always more intimidating than what is known.

- Seeing the room will enable you to plan possible contingencies that you may not otherwise have known about. For example, the room may be much larger or much smaller than you expected.

Videotape yourself.

- If you have access to a video camera, by all means use it to practice your presentation. There is nothing like video feedback to show you what you do well and where you could improve.

- Be sure to videotape yourself a second time after you've practiced a few more times. You'll see improvements and it will help your confidence.

Audiotape yourself and use the tape to practice.

- Audiotaping yourself as you practice is useful for the same reasons listed for videotaping.

- A second use of a practice audiotape is to play it in your car during the days before your presentation. It will help you memorize the key points of your talk, as well.

Practice using the equipment.

You have probably attended a seminar or workshop where the presenter fumbled with the VCR or microphones and became pretty embarrassed. Don't make the same mistake. It takes only a few minutes to practice using the equipment that's part of your presentation, even if it's as simple as a transparency projector.

6. *During the presentation.*

Introduce yourself.

Unless you're being introduced by someone else, be sure to state your name and what you do before you do anything else. It may seem obvious, but speakers have been known to omit this important piece of information.

Repeat questions.	Unless your meeting room is fairly small, it's courteous to repeat questions from people in the audience before you answer. Don't assume everyone heard every question.
Smile.	Even though you may be nervous, don't forget to smile. People want you to succeed. They usually are focusing much less attention on you than you think, and they usually just assume you know what you are talking about.
Look at one person at a time.	You will build the best rapport with your audience if you look at their faces and talk to them as individuals.
Breathe.	You will stay calmer if you remember to breathe.
Slow down.	If possible, have an ally in the audience who can signal you if you start talking too fast.
Answer questions.	Always set aside some time to find out what questions people have. Ask for questions with an open-ended question such as, "What questions do you have?" Then, be silent and allow people time to think and respond.
Say thank-you.	Always conclude your presentation by thanking the audience for their time and attention.

Exhibit 2.1 Types of Seating Arrangements

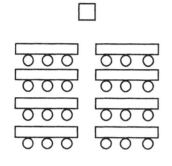

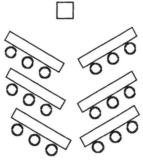

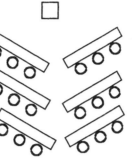

**Seminar
Arrangement
with Tables**
Effective seating for a fairly large group who will be taking notes; this is a very comfortable way to seat people for an all-day workshop where they will need to spread out.

**V-Shape with
Tables**
Effective seating for a fairly large group who will be taking notes; the V-shape enables the speaker to step into the audience and establish closer contact than with auditorium-style seating.

Auditorium
An effective arrangement for very large groups; works well for a lecture with minimal interaction.

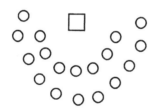

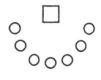

Double Semicircle
Enables the speaker to be closer to the audience members; allows more intimacy.

Semicircle
Provides a more intimate setting for a small group.

Chapter 3

12 Tips for Marketing

Your Practice

Why Should You Market Your Practice?

Let's talk about why marketing is a critical skill for a successful counseling or psychotherapy practice.

1. *To build your business.* The first reason to market is the most obvious: Most therapists in private practice want more clients. Marketing is a way to find those clients and get them to call you.
2. *To let people know you exist.* Marketing is a series of activities that will tell the people in your marketplace that you exist. Without marketing, how will people find out about you? There will always be a few therapists who will tell you they just opened their doors and people started calling, but these are the exceptions. The rest of us need to spend at least 50 percent of our time marketing.
3. *To have a road map.* When you design and implement a marketing campaign, you create a road map for yourself and your business. It gives you a sense of direction and something to measure results against. This gives most businesspeople a feeling of security and satisfaction, which is lacking when there is no plan.
4. *To understand where your business comes from,* so you can get more. A marketing program includes certain elements that all fit together. You will analyze your market, set goals, implement your plans, and measure the results of your efforts. As you begin to see results, you will understand what actions produced those results. You will know what actions to repeat to get more results. You will also know what actions failed to produce results, and you will not want to repeat them.

Now let's look at a few tips that should give you some direction in your marketing efforts.

Marketing Tip #1: Analyze the Marketplace

Can you imagine starting a new business without first understanding who lives in the area surrounding it? It's amazing, but many therapists do just that when they set up their first practice. Let's look at what such an analysis involves and why it's a crucial step.

Define your marketplace in terms of:

1. *Competition.* One important part of your market analysis is taking a look at the competition. Who else is practicing in your area? You will want to find out the following information:

   - How many other therapists are there within a 2- to 5-mile radius?
   - What licenses do these therapists hold? How many of each type of license?

- What can you learn about the practice specialties of these competitors?
- What kinds of marketing are your competitors doing?
- How visible are they? Are they more than just listings in the Yellow Pages?

It's a good idea to get in your car and take a drive. See what office buildings your competition is located in. Make notes. Mark their locations on a map. See where they cluster. What opportunities do you see?

2. *Demographics.* This data includes facts about the people who live in your area. It includes things like:

- Average age
- Income
- Education
- Occupation
- Marital status
- Gender
- Family size
- Percentage who are homeowners
- Average home price

This information can be found at places such as the following:

- The Chamber of Commerce
- The public library (ask the librarian)
- Local business publications
- Real estate offices

This information is important, especially when you are deciding where to open a practice. Many people consider psychotherapy to be an expensive service, and demographic factors will help you decide the most favorable locations to open such a business. It will also help you decide which specialty areas to market, based on the population living in your market area.

3. *Trends.* Current trends are important to consider when you are designing a marketing plan for your practice. Examples of trends are:

- More young families moving in
- Senior citizen population expanding
- Large companies expanding or downsizing
- Mergers and closings
- More of certain ethnic groups moving in
- Recent disasters (earthquakes, floods, hurricanes, tornadoes, etc.) that have impacted the economy as well as people's psyches

You can learn about such trends in the following ways:

- Read the paper.
- Surf the internet.
- Walk through the mall or down the street.
- Watch TV news shows.

Marketing Tip #2:
Know Your Competition

Understanding your competition is a very important element of your success. First, look in the Yellow Pages and other listings and be sure you understand who is out there vying for the same clients you are. Then you have to get creative. You want to find out what those competitors of yours are really like.

- How do they do business?
- How do they treat clients?
- What are their offices like?

One way to do this is to go "therapist shopping." It's a bit like being a mystery shopper in a department store. Choose a few therapists whom you'd like to know more about. Call their offices and ask if you can meet with them. Say you're doing a survey of the market area and you want to get to know the other practitioners. Make a list of questions you'd like to ask, such as:

- Hours of availability
- How they work with clients
- Areas of specialty
- Fees

If possible, visit each therapist. Note how you feel as you walk into the office building, the waiting room, and the therapy room. How might a client feel? What impression do you get as you meet with each person? What do you think he or she does particularly well?

Identify ways your practice is superior or unique. After you've met with a few of your competitors, make a list of what you've learned. What do most therapists do especially well? What opportunities do you see to excel? Evaluate your findings in terms of the following factors:

- How long licensed?
- Any special training?
- Specialty areas?
- Affordable fees?
- Comfortable, nonintimidating office?
- Feeling of safety in the parking lot and building?
- Conveys a feeling of confidence?
- Conveys a feeling of warmth?
- Office feels private?
- Confidential atmosphere; files are locked and conversations are private?

Find new ways to create more value for your clients. Consider the practice elements listed in this section. Think of the other therapists in your market area, and make a list of at least five ways you could create more value today for your clients.

Marketing Tip #3:
Know What Your Clients Value

In *The Guerrilla Marketing Handbook* (a must-read, along with the entire Guerrilla Marketing series), Jay Conrad Levinson and Seth Godin write that one key to success in your practice is to deliver more than the customer expects. They write, "Act on the knowledge that customers value attention, dependability, promptness, and competence" (page 348).

Compare yourself to your competition in terms of those four elements—attention, dependability, promptness, and competence—and find five ways to create more value for your clients. You will soon have more clients.

Here are a few things to consider:

1. *Concrete aspects of your service.* This includes things like the following:

   - The length of your sessions
   - Your fee
   - Insurance reimbursement; participation in managed care programs
   - How much information you provide your clients
   - What other services you offer besides counseling
   - What kinds of clients and issues you work well with

   You have made decisions about each of these aspects of your service. Do your decisions match what your clients value?

2. *Office location.* Think about the following:

   - How easy is the office to find?
   - Is there plenty of parking? Is it free?
   - Does it feel safe in the daytime and at night?
   - Is it accessible to people with disabilities?
   - Is it clean?
   - Is it comfortable and friendly?
   - Does it convey a professional feeling?

   Again, you have made decisions about each of these aspects of your service. Do your decisions match what your clients value?

3. *Time* is an important part of your service. Think about the following, and add your own items to the list.

   - How long are your sessions? Have you started seeing clients for less time at the same fee? How do you think the clients feel about this? What would happen if you did the opposite—perhaps offer 90-minute sessions at the original fee? Remember, those who give the client more than he or she expects will be the winners in this competitive climate.
   - Are you available when your clients are? Are you rigidly seeing clients once each week, or are you willing to be flexible and try new arrangements? What about seeing them every other week

with a 10-minute telephone touch base in between? It would mean one less trip to your office for your busy clients. Many of them might appreciate it.

- How quickly do you work? Are you willing to embrace the current methods of doing therapy and spend less time with each client? Have you asked your clients what they prefer?

4. *Convenience.* How easy do you make it for your clients to get what they need and want from you? Are there unnecessary barriers that may have gone unnoticed and that could be eliminated?

   For example: Therapist Gilda's only available hours are on Tuesdays and Saturdays. She works for a "therapy mill" (a large group practice) and is one of about 20 therapists on the staff. The only way for clients to reach her is through the practice, and they must always leave a message. There is no voice mail and no pager.

   The frustration created by this lack of availability is enormous. And so are the opportunities for the competition!

What are your own examples of how you could create more value for your clients than the competition does?

Marketing Tip #4:
Know What Makes You Unique

Why is it so important to stand out from the crowd? To give clients a reason to choose you instead of the many other therapists available—or instead of choosing the option of "do-it-yourself" therapy.

Always ask yourself, "Why would a client choose me?" Make a list of at least five ways that you are different from almost everyone else. Don't worry if they don't seem to relate to the business of psychotherapy. Here are some examples:

- Anne was born in Israel and speaks fluent Hebrew.
- Krystal spent 15 years as an executive recruiter before becoming a therapist.
- Steve is a cancer survivor.
- Susan is a registered dietician and licensed psychologist.
- Belinda is an adoptive parent.

Stress your unique points in every marketing effort. The point, of course, is to find several ways in which you are different from almost every other therapist—and emphasize those differences in your marketing campaign. Here is how the five therapists you just read about stressed their differences in their practices:

- Anne markets her counseling services to Israeli immigrants. She conducts many of her sessions in Hebrew.
- Krystal specializes in career counseling and offers a support group for survivors of corporate downsizing.
- Steve specializes in working with the families of people with serious illnesses.

- Susan specializes in working with clients with eating disorders.
- Belinda offers support groups for prospective adoptive parents.

Marketing Tip #5: Emphasize the Benefits of Your Services

To help you differentiate your counseling services from those of your competitors, you must learn to spell out the features and benefits. The first step is to define your service. Second, list the features your counseling service offers which are different from the services your competitors offer. Then, for each feature, identify the benefits of your service. Benefits answer the question, "Why is this important to me?"

Stress these benefits in all of your marketing efforts. Here is another way of looking at benefits: They answer the question, "How does my service make my client's life better?"

Marketing Tip #6: See Yourself from the Client's Perspective

What impression do you make? Being competitive means staying aware of how you come across to your clients, especially first impressions.

If you have recently shopped for a therapist for yourself or a family member, the experience may have been an eye-opener. Chances are, it reminded you that we must always be aware of how we come across to our clients—in so many ways.

1. *Through your written communications.* Be aware that your written communications—your business stationery, Yellow Pages ad, other ads, and so on—create an impression with potential clients. Do yours help you stand out from the crowd, or do they look like everyone else's?

    Look at your business cards. How are they similar from the business cards of other therapists? How are they different? What impact is each likely to make on a prospective client? The purpose here is not to be judgmental, but to learn about what makes an impact.

2. *During the first phone contact.* Recently when looking for a therapist, a client left a message requesting a return call to discuss starting therapy. When the therapist called back, it was obvious that she was holding a baby as she talked on the phone. The client could hear the baby gurgling in the background and the therapist even had to excuse herself once to shift the baby to another position.

    What is wrong with this therapist's behavior on the phone, and how is this related to marketing?

- The behavior is unprofessional and not businesslike.
- A client in distress may be distracted or upset by hearing a baby in the background.
- The therapist had no knowledge about this client. Consider the possibility that this client is infertile or has other issues that would make her especially sensitive to hearing a baby.

3. *In your waiting room.* A large, busy practice specializing in children's issues has a waiting room that is almost always overflowing with families. It is very noisy and chaotic. The magazines are strewn about with covers torn. This practice is in a fairly small town, so clients get the feeling that their problems are on public view. They often see other families from their school coming and going.

   The office staff members of this practice sit in a room next to the waiting room and make telephone calls to clients and other professionals within the hearing of the waiting clients. Names and medications are freely mentioned with no attempt at privacy.

   Aside from the ethical violations, what is wrong with this picture—from a *customer service* point of view?

- The client feels a lack of privacy.
- The chaotic waiting room adds to clients' anxiety.
- When overhearing the staff discussing other clients, waiting clients wonder how their own information is overheard.

4. *At the first meeting.* At a busy nonprofit counseling center, new clients coming for the first visit (called an *intake,* not a particularly customer-friendly term) are handed a clipboard with several pages of forms to fill out. The intake therapist rattles off a long series of questions and takes notes. What impression do you suppose this might make on the client?

   While information gathering is necessary, especially in the beginning, what negative impression might it create? How might this impression be softened? Be aware of the tendency to ask questions in a rote manner. Acknowledge to the client the possible negative feeling created by such questions. Perhaps you can think of a few more examples of ways therapists might create a negative impression during the first session.

Marketing Tip #7:
Identify Your Target Client

You may have heard the marketing term *target market.* Have you identified yours? Let's find out how this will help you build a strong practice. Most therapists market their services to two groups:

- People who will be their clients
- People or groups who will refer clients to the practice

This is an important distinction. Be sure to identify who belongs in each of these categories for your practice, and include them both in your marketing strategy. For example:

Target clients: People who are infertile
Referral sources: Reproductive endocrinologists

How do people choose a therapist? Here are a few typical ways:

- Consult a Yellow Pages ad.
- Ask their doctor or clergy.
- Ask the school psychologist.
- Ask a friend or relative.
- Attend a seminar or workshop given by a therapist.
- Consult a managed care list.

Most referrals are based on someone's knowledge about the therapist. Therefore, it is important that you:

- Make contact with as many potential referrers as you can—by networking.
- Make it as easy as possible for people to refer to you—by networking.
- Make it as easy as possible for potential clients to choose you—by being visible and active in your community.

Since the most important element in the choice of a therapist is trust, your key task is to make yourself as accessible as possible. What kinds of things would add to your accessibility? You could do things like these:

- Include your photo in your advertisements (Yellow Pages, newspaper, flyers, etc.).
- Participate in numerous networking events, for as long as you are in business.
- Offer to speak to groups.
- Give free seminars and events at your office or in hotel meeting rooms.

Marketing Tip #8:
Market to Your Target Client

A target client has certain specific traits, such as their demographic profile, geographic location, and type of lifestyle. Target marketing is different from general marketing in that you identify a specific segment or niche and design all of your marketing activities to appeal to clients belonging to that group. Examples of target clients include:

- Upper middle class, married, $75K income and above, living in zip code 91107, no children, age 30 to 39
- Middle class, divorced, single parents, $20K to $40K income, living in zip codes 91405 to 91407, age 25 to 40

How might the services for these two groups be different? Here are some possible ways:

- The first group would be most interested in couples groups, marital therapy, career issues, and workshops on personal growth issues.

- The second group would be interested in a workshop on survival skills for single parents, evening availability, family therapy, and brief therapy.

In *Rocking the Ages: The Yankelovich Report on Generational Marketing* (noted in the Resource List at the end of this chapter), authors J. Walker Smith and Ann Clurman describe how effective marketing campaigns can be designed based on understanding the generation to which the target client belongs: Generation X, the Baby Boomers, and what the authors call the Matures. The authors state that the values, preferences, and behaviors of consumers can be understood by understanding "three distinct elements: 1) life stage, 2) current social and economic conditions, and 3) formative cohort experiences." If you identify the generation of your target clients, you can better target your services to meet their needs and values.

Set your fees based on this client. When setting your fees, you should consider the following factors:

- What your competitors are charging
- What your clients consider a reasonable amount
- Trends in your area and in your profession
- Your target client

Fees are difficult to price because your service is intangible. Some experts say that those who purchase services see price as an indicator of quality, so a lower fee has a negative impact on how potential clients might see you.

In *The Guerrilla Marketing Handbook* (noted in the Resource List at the end of this chapter), Levinson and Godin write, "When a customer tells you that your price is too high, what he's really saying is, that you don't give enough value for what you're charging. Time and time again, aggressive businesses have shown that people will pay for quality and service. . . . Your price is rarely the problem. Worry instead about benefits, positioning, and service" (page 306).

Avoid the temptation to lose your focus. Building a successful practice takes a few years. When results are lacking, it is tempting to blame your marketing campaign and think about trying something different. If your program is based on a well-thought-out analysis, however, changing tracks may be the wrong move. It will certainly be confusing to your colleagues and referral sources.

Try the following instead:

- Talk it over with someone who can advise you.
- Consider making minor adjustments to your plan before you make any radical changes.
- Ask a few trusted friends or colleagues to help you brainstorm ways to get your business moving.

Marketing Tip #9: Develop a Marketing Plan and Short-Term Objectives

It is critical to write your plan down and refer to it often. You need both a long-range plan covering the next 1 to 3 years, and short-term objectives for the coming 6 to 12 months.

Objectives are effective only if they are written in language that is

- Specific
- Concrete
- Measurable

Update your objectives regularly. Once you've developed a killer set of objectives, don't stick them in the drawer and forget about them. Do just the opposite: Put them to work, and keep them up to date.

- Put them on your bulletin board right next to your desk.
- Make an action calendar with subgoals and checkoff lists.
- Reward yourself when you accomplish what you set out to do.

Marketing Tip #10:
Design a Promotional Strategy

A promotional strategy is a combination of activities designed to attract people's attention and get them to call for an appointment. How will people hear about you?

A promotional strategy is necessary because you need to have a plan for how people will find out about you. Just hanging out your shingle and hoping the phone will ring is not a strategy. Neither is "if I build it, they will come." A strategy is a set of actions designed to accomplish a specific goal.

Promotions include things like advertisements, public relations, and sales promotions. When deciding whether to advertise, consider your target market and special services you've developed for them. Choose the medium your target client is most likely to read.

Generate publicity by staging events such as your own seminars and workshops, and offering to speak to community groups. Develop a mailing list of media outlets—every one you can think of—and regularly send them press releases announcing your events and programs. *Guerrilla P.R.* by Michael Levine (see the Resource List) is an excellent resource.

A random promotional strategy will produce random results, at best. Most likely, such a strategy will produce no results at all.

Marketing Tip #11:
Measure the Results of Your Efforts

This tip may seem like an obvious one, but it is one of the most important points of this workshop. Let's look at why.

Therapist Sheila decides to run a few ads to get her practice going. In Week 1, she spends $78 to run a small but tasteful ad in the local paper. No calls. She thinks, I must need more time. So she spends another $78 on an ad during the second week. One call, but no appointment was scheduled. In Week 3, she decides that her ad isn't big enough. So she spends $132 for a larger ad. Again, one call, but no appointment. And in Week 4, she tries one more time. She just can't believe that the ads didn't produce anything. But she can't resist trying again. She thinks, maybe repetition is the key. After all, she sees so many other businesses with similar ads in the same paper, week after week. Maybe it takes a few months to make people notice me.

After 10 weeks, Sheila is out of money. What did she get for her ads? Three calls, and one scheduled a consultation. The client no-showed, by the way!

Interestingly, other therapists in town saw Sheila's ads. After a few weeks, they thought, this Sheila must be very successful if she can afford all of this advertising!

Analyze the Costs and Results of Each Marketing Activity

Let's assume that Sheila did have a marketing plan. She gave herself 4 weeks of ads at $78 per week. She saw that for the ads to pay off, she would need to produce at least 4 × $78, or $312 worth of business to break even. If her hourly fee was $80, she would need to see about four clients.

Do More of What Produces Results

The 80/20 rule, which is also known as the Pareto Principle, says that 80 percent of the results are produced by 20 percent of the resources. Applied to the business of psychotherapy, it means that 80 percent of the clients come from 20 percent of the referral sources. Know what your top 20 percent is and spend your energy making that grow.

Do Less of What Doesn't Produce Results

If an activity isn't producing results, stop doing it. Back to Sheila: We don't know enough about her ad to know why it didn't produce any clients. Perhaps the ad copy was the problem. Maybe the paper was the wrong place to advertise to attract the target client. Maybe Sheila never thought to target a client. But one thing is certain: If it wasn't working after the fourth week, she should have stopped what she was doing and tried something different.

Marketing Tip #12: Don't Give Up

Have you ever felt like giving up? It happens to all of us. It can be very discouraging, especially if you are a solo practitioner. But don't give up!

Allow enough time for your efforts to produce results. Building a successful practice takes a few years. There are no shortcuts. Expecting anything different is not being fair to yourself. If you are going to set out on this journey, you must be realistic in your estimate of how long it will take for success to come.

In another must-read, *Making It on Your Own,* Sarah and Paul Edwards devote an entire chapter to "Staying Up No Matter What Goes Down." Reading this book is like therapy for the discouraged private practitioner. The authors describe their own experiences with the fact that "success has a schedule of its own" (page 229).

Success is 99 percent persistence. I'm not sure who said it, but doesn't it seem true? Good things (success) come to those who persist.

What to Do When You Feel Like Quitting

Those who manage to hang on through the hard times when the phone isn't ringing and their only three clients cancelled must have a secret.

The following is a list of things you can do when you feel like quitting and going back to the career you left (because you hated it) before you became a therapist. Add your own ideas.

1. Spend some time with friends and colleagues who will tell you what a terrific therapist you are.
2. Reread your journal entries from the days when you were deciding to become a therapist.
3. Remember how much you disliked the career you had before you started graduate school.
4. Make a list of 20 reasons why you became a therapist.
5. Read the biographies of successful people. Note how most of them didn't become successful until they endured many failures and years of barely making it.
6. Write yourself a letter from the successful and satisfied professional you will be in five years and thank yourself for staying with it.

Keep your eye on your market. Remember, marketing goes on forever. It is an essential part of running your successful psychotherapy business. Never take your eye off your market.

Good luck. And luck *is* part of the equation.

Resource List

Beckwith, Harry. *Selling the Invisible: A Field Guide to Modern Marketing.* New York: Warner Books, 1997.

Edwards, Sarah and Paul. *Making It on Your Own: Surviving and Thriving on the Ups and Downs of Being Your Own Boss.* New York: Jeremy P. Tarcher, 1991.

Levine, Michael. *Guerrilla P.R.: How You Can Wage an Effective Publicity Campaign without Going Broke.* New York: HarperCollins, 1993.

Levinson, Jay, and Seth Godin. *The Guerrilla Marketing Handbook.* Boston: Houghton Mifflin, 1994.

Smith, J. Walker, and Ann Clurman. *Rocking the Ages: The Yankelovich Report on Generational Marketing.* New York: HarperCollins, 1997.

White, Sarah. *The Complete Idiot's Guide to Marketing Basics.* New York: Alpha Books, 1997.

Chapter 4

Before the Wedding:
Skills for Marriage
Success

Presentation Synopsis

This workshop is designed for couples who are planning to marry. It presents current research on marriage and outlines the skills needed to build a relationship that will be successful in the long term. You may wish to combine the content from other workshop outlines to suit the needs of specific groups.

This presentation is based, in part, on information from the following books. I recommend that you review them as you prepare your presentation:

Gottman, John. *The Seven Principles for Making Marriage Work.* New York: Crown, 1999.

Gottman, John. *Why Marriages Succeed or Fail and How You Can Make Yours Last.* New York: Fireside Books, 1994.

Markman, Howard, Scott Stanley, and Susan Blumberg. *Fighting for Your Marriage: Positive Steps for Preventing Divorce and Preserving A Lasting Love.* San Francisco: Jossey-Bass, 1994.

Subotnik, Rona, and Gloria Harris. *Surviving Infidelity: Making Decisions, Recovering from the Pain.* Holbrook, MA: Adams, 1994.

Wallerstein, Judith, and Sandra Blakeslee. *The Good Marriage: How and Why Love Lasts.* New York: Warner Books, 1995.

Time Requirements

This presentation runs from 1 hour to 3½ hours, depending on the style of the presenter and the number of interactive activities used.

🕐 **Clock symbol.** This means that the information is included for a longer seminar or workshop. Omit these sections for a shorter presentation. If time is limited, another way to shorten your presentation is to share the information in lecture format. However, keep in mind that it is often harder to engage and maintain the audience's interest with a pure lecture style. Unless you are a particularly dynamic speaker, you will probably want to keep at least a few of the exercises to enliven the presentation.

How to Use This Presentation

Possible Audiences	Whom to Contact
Young adult groups at churches and synagogues	Minister, rabbi, or director of adult education programs
Bridal store customers	Store manager or director of public relations
Single adults attending classes or workshops as part of community adult education programs	Director of community adult education programs

Sample Text for Marketing Letter, Brochure, or Postcard

Even though the marriage failure rate has been widely publicized, there are many successful marriages in the world today. Anyone thinking about or planning marriage can learn from those who are succeeding. As a community service, I am offering a low-cost workshop to the members of your organization/your customers called "Before the Wedding: Skills for Marriage Success."

In this workshop, participants will learn about the tasks every couple must accomplish in order to have a lasting marriage. They will learn specific skills needed to carry them through the challenges of daily life, and they will find out what behaviors have a deadly impact on a marriage. Through written exercises and group discussion, this workshop helps participants learn the skills needed for marriage success and opens a dialogue between couples before their wedding day.

_____ is a licensed _____ in private practice in _____. S/he specializes in _____ and _____. Call _____ today to schedule your group's **free** workshop. (_____) _____-_____.

Sample Text for Press Release

_____ Presents "Before the Wedding: Skills for Marriage Success"

_____ is presenting a **free** workshop on how to build a marriage that will last for years. The workshop is scheduled for _____, from _____ to _____ at _____. The workshop is limited to ____ participants and is open to the public.

This workshop will be conducted by _____, who states, "Just about everyone has heard that the divorce rate is around 50 percent. There are reasons for this, and there are things that couples can do to make their marriage last. In this workshop, participants will learn specific ways to make love last. They will also learn the most common reasons that marriages fail and how to make sure it doesn't happen to them."

_____ is a licensed _____ in private practice in _____. S/he specializes in _____ and _____. For reservations, call _____ at (_____) _____-_____.

Exhibit 4.1 Presentation Outline

Before the Wedding: Skills for Marriage Success

Topic	Time Estimate
I. Introduction	
A. Introduce yourself	1 minute
B. Ask group members to introduce themselves	10 minutes
C. State workshop goals	1 minute
II. Introduction to Research	
III. Wallerstein's Nine Tasks	10–30 minutes
A. Separate from family of origin	
B. Create a sense of "we-ness"	
C. Make the transition to parenthood	
D. Weather crises	
E. Manage conflict	
F. Maintain sexual relationship	
G. Share mutual interests	
H. Comfort and encourage each other	
I. Accept growing older	
IV. Gottman's Skills for Marriage Success	10–20 minutes
A. Conflict management skills needed	
B. Positive-to-negative ratio	
C. Stable equilibrium	
D. Conflict management skills	
E. Overlearning and practice	
V. Gottman's Marriage Destroyers	10–20 minutes
A. Criticism	
B. Contempt/video example	
C. Defensiveness/video example	
D. Stonewalling	
VI. Exploring Values	5–40 minutes
VII. Exploring Expectations	10–45 minutes
VIII. Exploring Responsibilities	2–20 minutes
IX. What's Next?	13 minutes
X. Conclusion	1 minute
Approximate Total Time	**63–201 minutes**

Exhibit 4.2 Presentation Script

Before the Wedding: Skills for Marriage Success

Outline	Presenter's Comments	Activity
I-A. **Introduce Yourself**	My name is _____. I'm a licensed _____, with a _____ in _____. I specialize in working with _____, and became interested in why some marriages succeed and others don't. I started noticing this _____ ago, when _____ _____ _____ _____.	Refer to your bio on the first page of the handouts.
I-B. **Group Intro** 🕐	I'd like to start things off today by finding out a bit about each of you. Let's go around the room. Would each of you please tell us your name and something about yourself? If your partner is here, you may also wish to tell us what plans you have for your relationship.	If time allows, ask participants to introduce themselves. 10 minutes
I-C. **Goals**	The purpose of today's workshop is to explore why some marriages succeed while others fail—and to help you identify the skills and behaviors that will help yours last forever. You will learn about two recent sets of studies that have been conducted by psychologists. You will learn what these researchers discovered, and you will find out how you can apply it to your own relationship.	State goals. 1 minute.
II. **Introduction to Research**	In the early 1990s, psychologist Judith Wallerstein coauthored a study with Sandra Blakeslee. This work is detailed in the popular book *The Good Marriage: How and Why Love Lasts.*	
III. **Wallerstein's Nine Tasks**	Wallerstein studied 50 couples who had been married an average of 21 years. Her goal was to learn why some marriages succeed while others fail. She hoped to find out how the people in good marriages differ from those in bad ones. Wallerstein found that to have a successful marriage, couples must complete nine tasks during their life together. Based on her interviews with the 50 couples, she determined that couples whose marriages are unsuccessful failed to	30 minutes. Handout 4.1. • Read each vignette. • Identify task. • Lead discussion.

4.5

Outline	Presenter's Comments	Activity

complete these tasks. Those who stayed happily married accomplished all nine of them.

Handout 4.1 includes nine vignettes that illustrate the problems that can result when each of the tasks is not completed. Let's read each vignette to learn about these important tasks.

III-A.
Separate from Family of Origin

Task #1 (*Read the vignette.*)

What task does this seem to illustrate?

(Answer: Each partner must separate emotionally from the family of his or her childhood.)

Each partner must separate emotionally from the family of his or her childhood. This allows the partners to invest fully in the marriage.

What are some signs that one of the partners might be a bit too attached to his or her family of origin?

Task #1.

- Read vignette.
- Identify task.
- Lead discussion.

Ask question.

Examples to provide if none are offered:

- Visiting too often
- Staying too long
- Making frequent phone calls
- Offering unsolicited advice
- Meddling

Present information as lecture if time is limited.

III-B.
Create a Sense of Togetherness

Task #2 (*Read the vignette.*)

What task does this seem to illustrate?

(Answer: At the beginning of the marriage, create a sense of togetherness and also autonomy)

At the beginning of the marriage, it is important to create a sense of togetherness and also autonomy. It means creating a shared vision of how you want to spend your lives together. Wallerstein calls it creating a sense of we-ness, a feeling that you are part of a couple.

Task #2.

- Read vignette.
- Identify task.
- Lead discussion.

III-C.
Make the Transition to Parenthood

Task #3 (*Read the vignette.*)

What task does this seem to illustrate?

(Answer: Makes a successful transition to parenthood.)

If you become parents, you will need to make a successful shift from being a couple to being a family. At the same time, it is critical to maintain your sense of separateness as a

Task #3.

- Read vignette.
- Identify task.
- Lead discussion.

Outline	Presenter's Comments	Activity
	couple. Wallerstein notes that "a significant number of divorces occur because the couple is not ready to integrate a child."	
	There are two parts to this task: the first is that as a parent, you must be able to put the needs of your child before your own. The second is that you must not become so involved with your children that you emotionally abandon your mate.	
III-D. **Weather Crises**	Task #4 (*Read the vignette.*)	Task #4.
	What task does this seem to illustrate?	• Read vignette. • Identify task.
	(*Answer: Take care of the relationship in times of crisis and adversity.*)	• Lead discussion.
	Wallerstein says that it is important to learn to face crises and adversity without allowing them to destroy your relationship with your partner. When there is a crisis in the family, like someone losing a job, a financial setback, or a tragedy of some kind, it creates emotional reactions among everyone involved. The stresses themselves, along with the reactions to the stresses, can be a huge strain on the relationship.	
	How you each cope with these crises will determine their impact on your relationship. Being able to maintain your perspective, not blaming the other, thinking ahead, and preventing things from becoming worse all help prevent disaster from taking over your marriage.	
III-E. **Manage Conflict**	Task #5 (*Read the vignette.*)	Task #5.
	What task does this seem to illustrate?	• Read vignette. • Identify task.
	(*Answer: Manage conflict effectively.*)	• Lead discussion.
	According to Wallerstein, successful couples learn to build a relationship where anger, conflict, and differences may safely be expressed. It has to be okay to have and express your own views.	
	It is important to recognize that conflict resolution is a set of skills that can be learned. Learn and practice these skills and your marriage will have a much greater chance of surviving and thriving.	
III-F. **Maintain Sexual Relationship**	Task #6 (*Read the vignette.*)	Task #6.
	What task does this seem to illustrate?	• Read vignette. • Identify task.
	(*Answer: Maintain your sexual relationship.*)	• Lead discussion.

Outline	Presenter's Comments	Activity
	This means not allowing the demands of work and the family to intrude.	
III-G. **Share Mutual Interests**	Task #7 (*Read the vignette.*) What task does this seem to illustrate? (*Answer: Share mutual interests, laughter, and fun; keep mutual interests alive.*)	Task #7. • Read vignette. • Identify task. • Lead discussion.
III-H. **Comfort and Encourage Each Other**	Task #8 (*Read the vignette.*) What task does this seem to illustrate? (*Answer: Comfort and encourage each other.*) All people need to have a safe place where they can be themselves and be vulnerable. A long-lasting marriage provides that place. This requires paying attention to the other person and knowing when he or she needs comfort.	Task #8. • Read vignette. • Identify task. • Lead discussion.
III-I. **Accept Growing Older**	Task #9 (*Read the vignette.*) What task does this seem to illustrate? (*Answer: Keep the romance in your relationship as you accept growing older.*) The final task is to keep a romantic and idealistic view of the relationship, while at the same time facing the reality that both partners are growing older and will never be young again.	Task #9. • Read vignette. • Identify task. • Lead discussion.
IV. **Gottman's Skills for Marriage Success**	Let's move on to our second expert view. John Gottman is a psychologist who has studied couples for 20 years. In his book *Why Marriages Succeed or Fail,* Gottman describes several of his studies that were designed to find out which behaviors lead to long-term success and which lead to divorce. His more recent book, *The Seven Principles for Making Marriage Work,* expands on the first work. You may wish to take notes on Handout 4.2.	Present information. 20 minutes with group participation. 10 minutes with no participation. Handout 4.2.
IV-A. **Needed: Conflict Management Skills**	The first finding outlined in Gottman's book is about style of dealing with conflict. He describes three styles: validating, conflict-avoiding, and volatile. All three kinds of marriages can be successful. The style isn't as important as learning how to manage conflict successfully.	

Outline	*Presenter's Comments*	*Activity*

**IV-B.
Positive-to-
Negative
Ratio**

The second finding is surprising in its simplicity. Gottman writes, "Amazingly, we have found that it all comes down to a simple mathematical formula: No matter what style your marriage follows, you must have at least five times as many positive as negative moments together if your marriage is to be stable."

**IV-C.
Stable
Equilibrium**

He continues, "If you and your spouse do not arrive at a stable equilibrium, when this balance, or 'marital ecology,' becomes upset, you and your mate will find yourselves frustrated, sniping or lost in a dead end, quarreling more and more. These are the signs of the failure to find a stable marital style that you both find comfortable" (page 29).

Ask the participants to comment on Gottman's finding that negative interactions must be balanced with a large number of positive interactions—in fact, the best ratio is 5:1.

What are some examples of positive interactions?

Ask for examples.

Examples to provide if none are offered:

1. Demonstrate that you are interested in your partner. Pay attention. ("You didn't sleep well last night, did you?")
2. Show affection.
3. Demonstrate that you care. Call and check in. ("How did the big negotiation go?")
4. Show appreciation. Let your partner know you are grateful for the relationship.
5. Express concern about events going on in your partner's life. ("How did your meeting turn out?")
6. Apologize for hurtful things you have said or done.
7. Show empathy. ("You seem upset")

By engaging regularly in these behaviors, you create a positive feeling in the relationship—an atmosphere of love and respect. This ties in with one of Wallerstein's tasks—comforting and encouraging each other. Doing these things helps you create a safe place where you can be yourself.

Present information.

To summarize this point about the 5:1 ratio, Gottman says, "If these rates are in balance, love thrives; when they get too far out of balance, then the love between a couple can start to wither and die, like an endangered species starved of its basic nutrients" (page 64).

Outline	Presenter's Comments	Activity
IV-D. **Four Conflict Management Skills**	Conflict is part of life. You and your partner will disagree about lots of things.	
	The important thing is how you and your partner respond to the conflict. Keeping in mind that a healthy marriage needs a large dose of positive interaction, it's important to know how to break the cycle of negativity when it starts.	
	Gottman recommends that you learn and practice four skills. They are listed on Handout 4.3:	Handout 4.3.
	1. Set a 15-minute discussion limit when you are in conflict. 2. Calm yourself and avoid flooding. 3. Speak and listen nondefensively. 4. Validate the other person.	
	Let's look at each of these skills.	
	The first skill is to set a 15-minute discussion limit when you are in conflict.	Present information and lead discussion.
	How would this help you manage conflict?	

Answer to look for:

Knowing that you have a 15-minute limit encourages you to get right to the point. Setting a timer is a good idea.

	How would this skill sound—what would you say or do?	Ask for an example.

Answer to look for:

"We have agreed to limit our discussions of things we disagree on to 15 minutes. If we haven't resolved it in 15 minutes, we'll take an hour's break and come back to it then. Let's set the timer and start now."

	The second skill is to calm yourself and avoid flooding (becoming overwhelmed with emotion). How would this help manage conflict?	Ask question.

Answers to look for:

- If you are calm, you are less likely to say things you'll later regret—things that could be destructive to your relationship.
- You will be less likely to become defensive and shut your partner out.

Outline	Presenter's Comments	Activity
🕐	What are some examples of ways to calm yourself and keep from getting carried away with emotion?	Ask for an example of skill.

Answers to look for:

- Pay attention to your physical responses. Is your heart racing? Are you breathing faster? If you are, take a 1-hour time out.
- Leave the room. Go for a drive. Do something relaxing. Listen to music or do relaxation exercises.
- Make a conscious effort to calm yourself down. Say things to yourself like,

"I'm very upset right now, but it'll be okay. I still love her."

"Even though we disagree, we still have a good relationship."

"We can work this out. We're partners."

	Presenter's Comments	Activity
	The next skill is to speak and listen nondefensively. Why is this important?	Ask why this is important.
🕐	**Answer to look for:** Being defensive creates a negative atmosphere. Acknowledging that two points of view exist creates an atmosphere of acceptance.	
	Take a moment to think of an example of this skill. What would you say or do to convey a nondefensive manner?	Ask for an example. 🕐

Here are some sample	**answers:**

- Show empathy for your partner. "I can see you're really upset."
- Acknowledge what your partner *has* done rather than focusing on what *hasn't* been done. "You did a good job of washing those dishes."
- Show appreciation for the good things your partner does. "You did a good job of working with Jeannie on her homework."
- Try to understand your partner's feelings, even if you don't agree with them. "I don't feel the same way, but I see why you're not happy with the money we spent."
- When you have a complaint, be specific. "I'm upset that you left the food out on the table."

Outline	Presenter's Comments	Activity

- Focus on the problem, not the person. "I wish you would take your stuff upstairs," not "You are such a complete slob."

The next skill is to validate the other person. This means letting your partner know that you understand him or her. It means showing empathy and understanding.

Ask why this is important.
Ask for examples.

Why is this important?

Answers to look for:

- Being validated feels good.
- It is a way to build up that 5:1 ratio of positive interactions.
- It makes you feel connected to your partner.

What is an example of validating?

Ask for examples.

Here are some sample answers:

- "I can see how angry that made you."
- "I'm sorry I did that. I really messed up your plans."
- "You handled that situation very well."

**IV-E.
Overlearning
and Practice**

These are skills that you can learn. You were *not* born knowing them. They will *not* come naturally to you and you will *not* feel natural using them in the beginning. But it's important to keep working on it.

Present information.

Author John Gottman advises that you practice these skills over and over. He calls this *overlearning*. He says (page 200), "if you overlearn a communication skill, you'll have access to it when you need it most—during an argument or heated fight." And that's when you will need it most.

**V.
Gottman's
Marriage
Destroyers**

According to Gottman, couples whose marriages fail gradually reach a point where "their emotional ecology is in trouble and their marriage is beginning to spin out of control." These couples slide into "a freefall toward destruction."

20 minutes with participation.

10 minutes with no participation.

Marriage counselors see these couples every day—couples who have fallen into a pattern of interaction marked by what Gottman calls "the four horsemen of the Apocalypse."

Outline	Presenter's Comments	Activity
	Gottman outlines four marriage-destroying behaviors: • Criticism • Contempt • Defensiveness • Stonewalling	Handout 4.4.
	These four behaviors are deadly to a marriage because they prevent productive communication from taking place. Let's look at each of them and learn how you can keep them out of your marriage. These are noted on Handout 4.4.	
V-A. Criticism	The first damaging behavior is criticism. Criticism involves "attacking someone's personality or character—rather than a specific behavior—usually with blame."	Present information.
	Criticism is different from a complaint. A complaint focuses on a specific action. Criticism is more blaming and more global.	Ask for an example.
	Can you think of an example of this behavior?	

Types of answers to look for:

"You always screw the budget up. Can't you do anything right?"

| | Why is this behavior damaging to a relationship? | Ask question. |

Answers to look for:

- Criticism is *destructive* rather than *constructive.*
- It involves blame.
- Criticisms are global and tend to be generalizations (*you always, you never,* etc.).
- Criticisms attack the other person personally.
- It feels overwhelming to be on the receiving end.

V-B. Contempt	The second deadly behavior is contempt. This is what happens when negativity goes unchecked and unresolved. Your negative thoughts and beliefs about your partner grow and escalate into abusiveness. Contempt involves "the intention to insult and psychologically abuse" your spouse.	Present information.
	That sounds awful, doesn't it? It *is* awful—that's why Gottman calls it one of the "four horsemen" in a marriage.	
	What are some examples of contemptuous behavior?	Ask for examples of contempt.

Outline	Presenter's Comments	Activity
🕐	**Answers to look for:** Answers that include behavior (verbal or nonverbal) involving a lack of respect. This can include insults, making faces, calling names, and so on.	
🕐 **Video Example**	Throughout Woody Allen's 1998 movie *Deconstructing Harry,* the characters played by Kirstie Alley and Judy Davis provide many examples. (Be sure to preview this before you show it. It is not suitable for all groups.) Other examples may be found in *Who's Afraid of Virginia Woolf.*	View video.
	Why is contempt so damaging?	Ask question.
🕐	**Suggested answer:** When a relationship is overtaken by abusiveness and negativity, how can it survive, let alone flourish?	
V-C. Defensiveness	Earlier in today's workshop, we talked about the third dangerous behavior, defensiveness. Defensiveness is an understandable reaction when you are in a conflict situation, but it's dangerous because it tends to escalate the conflict. Being defensive never helps resolve a conflict.	
	What are some examples of this behavior?	Ask for an example.
🕐	**Answers to look for:** • Denying responsibility (*I did not!*) • Making excuses (*I couldn't help it; traffic was awful.*) • Ignoring what your partner says and throwing a complaint back (*Yeah, well, what about the mess you left yesterday?*) • Saying "*Yes, but . . .*" • Whining • Rolling your eyes or making a face	
🕐 **Video Example**	Midway through Woody Allen's *Hannah and Her Sisters,* the characters played by Mia Farrow and Michael Caine argue about his unhappiness in their marriage. He is very defensive.	View video example.
	Why is this behavior so damaging to a relationship?	Ask question.
🕐	**Answer to look for:** Defensive behavior is dangerous because it tends to escalate the conflict. Being defensive never helps resolve a conflict.	

Outline	Presenter's Comments	Activity
V-D. Stonewalling	Stonewalling is the fourth marriage-destroying behavior. It means shutting the other person out. When it becomes a regular pattern of communication, stonewalling is very damaging to a relationship.	
	What is stonewalling?	Ask for an example.
	Answer to look for: Refusing to communicate, storming out of the room, any kind of withdrawing.	
	Why is stonewalling so damaging to a relationship?	Ask question.
	Answer to look for: Communication is impossible when one person refuses to participate. Stonewalling also is a negative behavior that only steers couples off track.	
VI. Exploring Values	Now that we've looked at the research on what leads to a long-lasting and happy marriage, let's talk about something else: the importance of exploring your values.	Handout 4.5— 40 minutes with participation; 5 minutes without.
	Take 15 minutes to complete Handout 4.5. (If time is limited, you may wish to make this a postworkshop exercise.)	Complete individually.
	Then allow another 15 minutes to compare notes with your partner. How were your answers similar and different?	Couples discuss in pairs.
	Now I have some questions for everyone in the group:	Lead group discussion.
	1. Did you all find that you agreed on everything? (Of course not.) What kinds of differences did you find?	
	2. Why is it important to talk about the differences?	
	3. Is conflict inevitable? (Yes!)	
	4. What have you already learned about conflict in marriage? (The important thing is to learn to manage conflict productively.)	
VII. Exploring Expectations	When couples marry, they make a set of agreements with each other. Many times, these agreements are not verbalized; they may be assumptions that each partner makes about how the marriage will be.	5 minutes.
	What kinds of agreements are we talking about here?	Ask question.

Outline	Presenter's Comments	Activity

🕐

Answers to look for:

- Rules about how we will treat each other
- Who will do what
- What kind of life we will have
- How we will handle money
- If and when we will have children

🕐

Is it better to talk about these things, or is it okay to assume that you will agree on them without talking about them?

Ask question.

🕐

Answer to look for:

It can be hard to talk about differences, but it is always better to bring them out in the open. *Not* talking about them prevents you from understanding what each other wants and creates potential for conflict.

Handout 4.6 provides an opportunity to bring the terms of your agreement out into the open.

Handout 4.6—
40 minutes with participation; 5 minutes without.

Please take 15 minutes to complete Handout 4.6. (If time is limited, this exercise may be completed after the workshop.)

Complete individually.

Then take another 15 minutes to compare and discuss what you wrote with your partner.

Couples discuss in pairs.

What kinds of differences did you discover?

Lead group discussion.

VIII. Exploring Responsibilities

🕐

One of the potential areas of conflict in a new marriage is deciding who handles the responsibilities of everyday life. Handout 4.7 is an exercise that will help you find out where you agree and where you may still have some things to work out.

Handout 4.7—
20 minutes with participation; 2 minutes without.

Take 5 to 10 minutes to complete this exercise. (If time is limited, participants may complete it after the workshop.)

Complete exercise.

When you are ready, exchange papers with your partner and compare each item. Take about 10 minutes for this discussion with your partner.

Discuss in pairs.

Who would like to describe what differences you and your partner discovered?

Discuss in group.

Outline	Presenter's Comments	Activity
IX. **What's Next?**	Handout 4.8 is the final exercise of today's workshop. Take 10 minutes to complete this exercise on your own and then 5 more to discuss it with your partner. Who would like to share what you wrote?	Handout 4.8—13 minutes. Complete and share with partner. Lead brief group discussion.
X. **Conclusion**	I hope you have enjoyed today's workshop. In the time remaining, I would be happy to answer any questions you may have.	Conclude the workshop.

Handout 4.1 The Nine Tasks of a Successful Marriage

According to Judith Wallerstein, people in successful marriages complete nine tasks throughout their lifetimes. If these tasks are not successfully completed, the couple's chances of long-term happiness are lessened. Each of these vignettes illustrates one of the nine tasks when it has not been completed.

Sheilah and Matt have been married 5 years. They have constant arguments over the role that Matt's mother plays in their lives. She comes over to their house at least three times each week and often calls Matt at work with comments about the way the house looks, advice about things, and suggestions about the children. Sheilah feels like Matt pays more attention to his mother than he does to her. She also senses her mother-in-law's disapproval.

Task #1: _____

Tanya and Jake are very busy with demanding careers. They hardly see one another anymore. Besides traveling extensively for her job, Tanya is involved in three volunteer organizations and goes to church every Sunday. Jake also travels and likes to spend as much time as he can on his boat each weekend. They both say they feel like ships passing in the night.

Task #2: _____

Michelle and Jim are the parents of 2-year-old Tiffany. They began having Tiffany sleep in their bedroom when she was a newborn and never moved her into her own room. Jim complains because Michelle spends all of her time with Tiffany and they never have any time alone together anymore. Since Michelle stays at home with their daughter, money is tight and they are reluctant to hire a sitter. They haven't been out alone as a couple since Tiffany was born.

Task #3: _____

Ed lost his job during a recent wave of downsizing in the insurance industry. He has been unemployed for 9 months now and it is taking a toll on the family. His wife, Marie, earns a good salary, but it isn't enough. He has become very depressed and angry. She was sympathetic and supportive at first, but since he has become so irritable, she has started avoiding him. Between the economic hardship and the way he has changed, she is ready to leave him.

Task #4: _____

Sarah and Rich never argue. She resents him tremendously because if she disagrees with him, he blows up at her and is hostile toward her for days. She has learned to keep her opinions to herself just to keep the peace. He thinks she is perfectly happy because there is peace in the house, but in fact she is counting the days until their son leaves for college so she can leave, too.

Task #5: _____

Linda and Mike had a satisfying sexual relationship for the first 3 years of their marriage. Then, when their children were born, they gradually stopped finding time for sex. Between being exhausted most of the time and feeling like they have no privacy, they haven't had sex for a year now.

Task #6: _____

John and Jane are living in the same house, but they live parallel lives. They have separate sets of friends and never go out together as a couple. Jane feels criticized by John whenever she speaks to him; in fact, he makes fun of her and mimics her. He seems annoyed whenever she tries to speak with him. She has given up asking him to join her in activities because he criticizes everything she suggests.

Task #7: _____

Sandy lost her job 3 months ago but hasn't told her husband, Will, about it yet. She gets up and goes out every morning, but Will doesn't realize that she isn't going to her office. She is afraid to tell him because she thinks he will be disappointed and angry at her, and she can't bear to add his feelings to her own shame.

Task #8: _____

Pete is about to turn 40. When he looks in the mirror, he sees an old man. Beth, his wife, is also about to turn 40. He wishes she would pay more attention to her appearance and color her hair the way her friends do. Seeing her looking older reminds him of his own aging. He feels sad about his lost youth and is thinking about joining a health club.

Task #9: _____

Source: The nine tasks are described in Judith Wallerstein and Sandra Blakeslee, *The Good Marriage: How and Why Love Lasts* (New York: Warner Books, 1995).

Handout 4.2   Why Marriages Succeed or Fail

1. John Gottman concluded that:

   • Style _____

   • Interactions must be _____

2. Examples of positive interaction:

   • _____

   • _____

   • _____

   • _____

   • _____

   • _____

   • _____

   • _____

Source: Reprinted with the permission of Simon & Schuster from *Why Marriages Succeed or Fail* by John Gottman, PhD. Copyright © 1994 by John Gottman.

Handout 4.3 Four Skills to Build Your Marriage

The following skills help break the cycle of negativity:

1. Set a 15-minute discussion limit.

   Example: _____

   Why this is important:

   _____

   _____

2. Calm yourself and avoid flooding.

   Example: _____

   Why this is important:

   _____

   _____

3. Speak and listen nondefensively.

   Example: _____

   Why this is important:

   _____

   _____

4. Validate the other person.

   Example: _____

   Why this is important:

   _____

   _____

It is important to practice the skills until they become automatic because _____

_____.

Source: Reprinted with the permission of Simon & Schuster from *Why Marriages Succeed or Fail* by John Gottman, PhD. Copyright © 1994 by John Gottman.

Handout 4.4 Four Marriage Destroyers

In *How Marriages Succeed or Fail,* author John Gottman found that the following four behaviors were the most damaging to marriages:

1. Criticism

   How it differs from a complaint: _____

   Example: _____

   Why it is so damaging:

   _____

   _____

2. Contempt

   Example: _____

   Why it is so damaging:

   _____

   _____

3. Defensiveness

   Example: _____

   Why it is so damaging:

   _____

   _____

4. Stonewalling

   Example: _____

   Why it is so damaging:

   _____

   _____

Source: Reprinted with the permission of Simon & Schuster from *Why Marriages Succeed or Fail* by John Gottman, PhD. Copyright © 1994 by John Gottman.

Handout 4.5 What Do You Value?

Circle the 10 values that are most important to you.

Achievement	Honesty
Activity	Independence
Admiration	Informality
Beauty	Learning
Being challenged	Leisure
Being recognized	Making a difference
Being well paid	Mastery
Belonging	Money
Calm	Morality
Certainty	Nature
Choice	Novelty
Comfort	Originality
Community service	Peace
Competition	Pleasure
Creativity	Power
Enjoyment	Prestige
Ethics	Privacy
Excitement	Reaching my potential
Expressing my uniqueness	Relaxation
Fame	Respect
Fitness	Safety
Flexibility	Security
Fortune	Solitude
Freedom	Spirituality
Friendship	Stability
Fun	Status
Growth	Time for family
Harmony	Time for friends
Health	Variety
Helping others	Wisdom

What do you believe about the following:

1. Religion and spirituality _____

_____

2. Family _____

_____

3. Children _____

_____

4.23

4. Marriage _____

_____

5. Fidelity _____

_____

6. Divorce _____

_____

7. Work _____

_____

8. Money _____

_____

9. Celebrations and holidays _____

_____

10. Commitment_____

_____

When you have completed this exercise, take some time to discuss it with your partner. Ask each other questions to clarify what each of you has written. Be careful not to criticize or judge each other's choices.

Here are some discussion questions:

1. In what ways are the two of you similar?

_____

_____

2. How are you different?

_____

_____

3. What are potential areas of conflict?

_____

_____

4. How can you and your partner support one another in living a life together that reflects both of your values?

_____

_____

Handout 4.6 My Expectations

It is important to explore and discuss your expectations with your partner *before* you begin your marriage. For each of the following items, describe your expectations, as well as the type of behavior you would *not* accept. *Be as specific as possible.* Then discuss them with your partner. Keep in mind that it is important to discuss each partner's expectations with the goal of understanding and clarifying each other's views. Be careful to avoid criticizing or judging each other.

I expect the following from my marriage partner:

1. I expect my partner to behave toward me . . .

   What I expect: _____

   _____

   What is not acceptable: _____

   _____

2. I hope others perceive my partner . . .

   What I expect: _____

   _____

   What is not acceptable: _____

   _____

3. I expect our sexual relationship . . .

   What I expect: _____

   _____

   What is not acceptable: _____

   _____

4. Our emotional relationship . . .

   What I expect: _____

   _____

   What is not acceptable: _____

   _____

5. As my companion . . .

What I expect: _____

_____

What is not acceptable: _____

_____

6. When we become parents . . .

What I expect: _____

_____

What is not acceptable: _____

_____

7. I expect to pursue my career and earn . . .

What I expect: _____

_____

What is not acceptable: _____

_____

8. I expect my partner to pursue a career and earn . . .

What I expect: _____

_____

What is not acceptable: _____

_____

9. I expect to manage our money . . .

What I expect: _____

_____

What is not acceptable: _____

_____

10. The atmosphere in our home . . .

What I expect: _____

_____

What is not acceptable: _____

_____

11. Our relationship with our parents and siblings . . .

What I expect: _____

_____

What is not acceptable: _____

_____

12. Other expectations: _____

What I expect: _____

_____

What is not acceptable: _____

_____

Handout 4.7   Whose Responsibility Is It?

The following is a list of tasks and chores that every couple manages. Decide who is responsible for each by checking in the appropriate column.

		Who Is Responsible?	
Task	**Wife**	**Husband**	**Either/Both**
Balance checkbook	_____	_____	_____
Buy holiday and birthday presents	_____	_____	_____
Choose and buy furniture for house	_____	_____	_____
Clean house	_____	_____	_____
Cook meals	_____	_____	_____
Do dishes	_____	_____	_____
Do laundry	_____	_____	_____
Drop off and pick up at cleaners	_____	_____	_____
Feed animals	_____	_____	_____
Maintain garden and lawn	_____	_____	_____
Make dentist appointments	_____	_____	_____
Make doctor appointments	_____	_____	_____
Make household repairs	_____	_____	_____
Make plans to see family members	_____	_____	_____
Make plans to see friends	_____	_____	_____
Make reservations for dinners	_____	_____	_____
Make vacation arrangements	_____	_____	_____
Make vacation plans	_____	_____	_____
Pay bills	_____	_____	_____
Send birthday cards	_____	_____	_____
Send holiday cards	_____	_____	_____
Set up holiday decorations	_____	_____	_____
Take down holiday decorations	_____	_____	_____
Take garbage cans to the curb	_____	_____	_____

Handout 4.8   What's Next?

1. What are the five most important things you have learned today about how to make your marriage succeed?

   - _____
   - _____
   - _____
   - _____
   - _____

2. What five actions do you plan to take to begin building a marriage that lasts forever?

   - _____
   - _____
   - _____
   - _____
   - _____

3. What five actions will you ask your partner to take?

   - _____
   - _____
   - _____
   - _____
   - _____

4. What are three things you want to know more about?

   - _____
   - _____
   - _____

5. How will you learn about them?

   - _____
   - _____
   - _____
   - _____

Chapter 5

The Good Marriage: Skills for Making Your Marriage Thrive

Presentation Synopsis

This workshop is designed for couples who have been married for 1 year or longer. It outlines the skills that will increase the likelihood of a long-lasting marriage, emphasizing two important areas: developing strong communication skills and knowing how to resolve conflict. In this workshop participants will learn about both of these sets of skills.

This presentation is based, in part, on information drawn from the following books. I recommend that you review them as you prepare your presentation:

Alberti, Robert, and Michael Emmons. *Your Perfect Right,* 7th ed. Atascadero, CA: Impact, 1995.

Burley-Allen, Madelyn. *Managing Assertively: A Self-Teaching Guide,* 2d ed. New York: John Wiley & Sons, 1995.

Burley-Allen, Madelyn. *Listening: The Forgotten Skill,* 2d ed. New York: John Wiley & Sons, 1995.

Gordon, Thomas. *Leader Effectiveness Training.* New York: Bantam Doubleday Dell, 1986.

McKay, Matthew, Peter Rogers, and Judith McKay. *When Anger Hurts: Quieting the Storm Within.* Oakland, CA: New Harbinger, 1989.

Rosellini, Gayle, and Mark Worden. *Of Course You're Angry,* 2d ed. Center City, MN: Hazelden Foundation, 1997.

Staheli, Lana. *Affair-Proof Your Marriage: Understanding, Preventing and Surviving an Affair.* New York: HarperCollins, 1995.

Tavris, Carol. *Anger: The Misunderstood Emotion.* New York: Touchstone, 1989.

Time Requirements

This presentation runs from 2 to 2½ hours, depending on the style of the presenter and the number of interactive activities used.

🕐 **Clock symbol.** This means that the information is included for a longer seminar or workshop. Omit these sections for a shorter presentation. If time is limited, another way to shorten your presentation is to share the information in lecture format. However, keep in mind that it is often harder to engage and maintain the audience's interest with a pure lecture style. Unless you are a particularly dynamic speaker, you will probably want to keep at least a few of the exercises to enliven the presentation.

How to Use This Presentation

Possible Audiences

Adult education groups at churches and
synagogues

PTO/PTA

Civic and professional organizations

Whom to Contact

Director of adult education programs

PTO/PTA president

Director of educational programs

Sample Text for Marketing Letter, Brochure, or Postcard

Most adults engage in long-term relationships, including marriage and other committed partnerships. Nearly everyone experiences difficulties in their marriage or committed relationship from time to time, but some people seem more prepared to anticipate these hard times and respond to them more skillfully than others. The skills that make a marriage last can be learned, and "The Good Marriage: Skills for Making Your Marriage Thrive" workshop provides an introduction.

_____ is offering this educational and motivational seminar to your group as a community service. In this workshop, participants learn several skills that will help them build and strengthen their marriages and long-term partnerships, including communication, listening and conflict management skills.

_____ is a licensed _____ in private practice in _____. S/he specializes in _____ and _____. Call _____ today to schedule your group's **free** workshop. (_____) _____-_____.

Sample Text for Press Release

_____ Presents "The Good Marriage: Skills for Making Your Marriage Thrive"

_____ is presenting a **free** workshop on how to build a thriving marriage or long-term committed relationship. The workshop is scheduled for _____, from _____ to _____ at

_____. It is designed for people who have been in their marriage or relationship for one year or more and is limited to ____ participants. It is open to members of _____ and the public.

According to _____, "A long-term lasting marriage or other committed relationship has certain characteristics that cause it to thrive. One of those characteristics is that the people in the relationship are skilled at communication and know how to manage conflict. In this workshop, we will explore a few of the skills that anyone can learn for a positive impact on their marriage."

_____ is a licensed _____ in private practice in _____. S/he specializes in _____ and _____. For reservations, call _____ at (_____) _____-_____.

Exhibit 5.1 Presentation Outline

The Good Marriage: Skills for Making Your Marriage Thrive

Topic	*Time Estimate*
I. **Introduction**	2–12 minutes
A. Introduce yourself	
🕐 B. Ask group members to introduce themselves	
C. State workshop goals	
II. **Importance of Communication**	21–37 minutes
🕐 A. Barriers to communication	
🕐 B. 12 communication roadblocks	
C. Why roadblocks hinder communication	
III. **Empathy and Acceptance**	5 minutes
IV. **Active Listening**	17 minutes
A. Why active listening is a valuable skill	
B. Why active listening is good for a marriage	
C. More active listening examples	
D. Active listening practice	
V. **Additional Listening Skills**	20 minutes
A. Open-ended questions	
B. Summary statements	
C. Neutral questions and phrases	
D. Listening skills: Practice exercises	
VI. **Assertive Communication**	5 minutes
VII. **Giving and Receiving Constructive Feedback**	18 minutes
A. You-messages	
B. I-messages	
VIII. **Resolving Conflicts**	10 minutes
IX. **Managing Anger**	15 minutes
A. Time-out	
B. Make a contract	
C. Ask questions	
D. Positive statements	
E. Prepared response	
X. **Business Skills for Marriages**	10 minutes
XI. **What's Next?**	2–8 minutes
🕐	
XII. **Conclusion**	
Approximate Total Time	**125–157 minutes**

Exhibit 5.2   Presentation Script

The Good Marriage: Skills for Making Your Marriage Thrive

Outline	Presenter's Comments	Activity
I-A. **Introduce Yourself**	My name is _____. I'm a licensed _____, with a _____. I specialize in working with _____, and became interested in why some marriages last a lifetime and others fall apart. I started noticing this _____ ago, when _____ _____.	Refer to your bio on the first page of the handouts. 1 minute.
I-B. **Group Intro** ⏲	I'd like to start things off today by finding out a bit about each of you. Let's go around the room and have each person tell us: • Your name • How long you've been married • The easiest thing about being married • The hardest thing about being married	If the group is under 20 people, ask participants to introduce themselves. 10 minutes.
I-C. **Goals**	This workshop is designed for couples who have been married or in committed relationships for one year or longer. This is what you will learn: • Some of the key skills needed for a successful marriage • The importance of developing strong communication skills • The importance of knowing how to resolve conflict • How to apply the skills of business to your marriage	State goals. 1 minute.
II. **Importance of Communication**	Any marriage counselor will tell you that one of the biggest problems they see when couples come for help is poor communication skills. People get into trouble in their marriages because they have not developed their ability to listen and communicate. In fact, in her book *Affair-Proof Your Marriage,* author Lana Staheli says that "a marriage can only be as good as the communication" (page 205). Let's begin our workshop with this important subject.	Introduce subject. 1 minute.

Outline	Presenter's Comments	Activity
II-A. **Barriers to Communica-tion** 🕐	Why do people not communicate effectively? What do you think the barriers are?	Ask question. 1–2 minutes.

Examples to provide if none are offered:

- Not knowing how to communicate properly
- Not taking the time to think through what you want to say
- Not taking the time to anticipate what your partner might be thinking and feeling
- Fear of revealing too much of yourself
- Fear of your partner's anger
- Not wanting to hurt your partner's feelings

(Activity column, aligned with II-A) If time is limited, present this information as a lecture.

Outline	Presenter's Comments	Activity
II-B. **12 Communi-cation Roadblocks** 🕐	In his classic book *Leader Effectiveness Training,* author Thomas Gordon lists 12 ways people often communicate— ineffectively. These are very common ways of attempting to gain control and solve a problem, but they are in fact roadblocks to effective communication. These 12 roadblocks are listed on Handout 5.1.	Handout 5.1.

Let's look at each roadblock. I'll give you one example of each and ask you to think of other examples. You may want to take notes on the handout.

1. Ordering, directing, and commanding.

   Example: You must be home by 5 P.M.

2. Warning, admonishing, and threatening.

   Example: You had better do it, or I'll be furious.

3. Moralizing, preaching, and imploring.

   Example: You should do this.

4. Advising and giving suggestions or solutions.

   Example: I really think you should do it this way.

5. Persuading with logic, lecturing, and arguing.

   Example: Your way makes no sense at all.

6. Judging, criticizing, disagreeing, and blaming.

   Example: I can't believe you wore that.

7. Praising, agreeing, evaluating positively, and buttering up.

   Example: You are such a competent person.

(Activity column, aligned with II-B roadblocks) Read roadblocks. Give examples. If time allows, ask for other examples. 10–25 minutes.

8. Name calling, ridiculing, and shaming.

   Example: You have no sense of direction.

9. Interpreting, analyzing, and diagnosing.

   Example: You're saying this because you're jealous.

10. Reassuring, sympathizing, consoling, and supporting.

    Example: You'll feel better tomorrow.

11. Probing, questioning, and interrogating.

    Example: How do you know it will work?

12. Distracting, diverting, and kidding.

    Example: You think that's bad? Wait till I tell you about *my* operation.

**II-C.
Why
Roadblocks
Hinder
Communication**

What's the problem with these messages?

Ask question.

1 minute.

Answer to look for:

They all convey the desire to change rather than accept the other person. They all communicate a desire for the other person to think, feel, or behave differently. This means they communicate *lack of acceptance.*

A climate of lack of acceptance is not conducive to personal growth and emotional well-being.

Present information.

8 minutes.

When people feel judged, threatened, put down, or analyzed, they feel defensive and resistant to change—especially when it's in their marriage. Such a climate also inhibits self-expression and self-exploration—both of which are necessary for solving one's own problems.

Finally, these statements take the responsibility for change away from the owner of the problem and place it in the hands of the speaker. It is important to keep the accountability focused on the person who owns the problem.

**III.
Empathy and
Acceptance**

People marry because they want to spend the rest of their lives with their partner. They have every hope of growing together and creating a relationship that makes them feel emotionally healthy. Again, in *Leader Effectiveness Training,* Thomas Gordon says that at least two ingredients are necessary for a relationship to be healthy: empathy and acceptance.

Present information.

5 minutes.

Outline	*Presenter's Comments*	*Activity*
	How would you define empathy?	Ask question.

Answer to look for:

Empathy is the capacity to put yourself in the other's shoes and understand how they view their reality; how they feel about things.

Demonstrating empathy and acceptance is critical to maintaining a strong relationship. Now we are going to look at some communication skills that enable you to create a climate of empathy, acceptance and understanding. We'll start with a skill called *active listening.*

| **IV.**
Active
Listening | Active listening is a way of communicating that creates the important climate of empathy, acceptance, and understanding. | Present information.
8 minutes. |

In *Affair-Proof Your Marriage,* the book I mentioned earlier, author Lana Staheli says that "active listening may be the most important single skill you can use. It is the basis for all types of intimate communication" (page 205).

- It is a two-step response to a statement made by your partner.
- It includes reflecting back what emotion you detected in the statement, and the reason for the emotion.

This is what active listening sounds like:

Sounds like you're upset about what happened at work.

You're very annoyed by my lateness, aren't you?

| **IV-A.**
Why Active
Listening Is a
Valuable Skill | Active listening is a valuable skill because it demonstrates that you understand what your partner is saying and how he or she is feeling about it. | |

- Active listening means restating, in your own words, what the other person has said.
- It's a check on whether your understanding is correct.
- It demonstrates that you are listening and that you are interested and concerned.

| | Does actively listening mean you have to agree with the other person? | Ask question. |

Answer:

No. The point is to demonstrate to your partner that you intend to hear and understand his or her point of view.

Outline	Presenter's Comments	Activity
IV-B. **Why Active Listening Is Good for a Marriage**	Why would this be good for your relationship?	Ask question.
	Answers to look for: • When someone demonstrates that they want to understand what you are thinking and feeling, it feels good. • It creates good feelings about the other person. • Restating and checking understanding promotes better communication and fewer misunderstandings.	
IV-C. **More Active Listening Examples**	Here are some more examples of active listening: *You sound really stumped about how to solve this problem.* *It makes you angry when you find errors on Joey's homework.* *Sounds like you're really worried about Wendy.* *I get the feeling you're awfully busy right now.*	Present information. 1 minute.
IV-D. **Active Listening Practice**	Handout 5.2 will give you some practice with active listening. Please complete this practice exercise. Now let's go over the exercise together. There is no one set of correct answers. Our goal is to make certain that your answers have both components of an active listening response, stating (1) the feeling being expressed and (2) the reason for the feeling.	Handout 5.2. Complete exercise. Discuss answers. 8 minutes.
V. **Additional Listening Skills**	Let's move on to some more listening skills. They are summarized on Handout 5.3. These skills enable you to demonstrate that you are interested in what the other person has to say. You will also learn to demonstrate that you are hearing and understanding your partner.	Handout 5.3. Present information. 10 minutes.
V-A. **Open-Ended Questions**	*Open-ended questions* begin with *what, why, how do,* or *tell me.* • These questions get the other person to open up and elaborate on the topic. • Asking these kinds of questions gets the other person involved by giving him or her a chance to tell what he or she thinks or knows.	

Outline	Presenter's Comments	Activity

- These questions are designed to encourage your partner to talk.
- They are useful when the other person is silent or reluctant to elaborate.
- They are also useful in dealing with negative emotions (such as anger or fear), since they help encourage the other person to vent feelings.

**V-B.
Summary
Statements**

Summary statements sum up what you hear your partner saying.

- A summary statement enhances your partner's self-esteem by showing that you were listening carefully.
- It also helps you focus on facts, not emotions.
- It helps your partner clarify his or her own thinking by hearing your summary.
- Summary statements also help you deal with multiple disagreements so you can deal with them one by one.
- They help eliminate confusion by focusing on the relevant facts.
- Summary statements also help you separate the important issues from the trivial.

**V-C.
Neutral
Questions
and Phrases**

Neutral questions and phrases get your partner to open up and elaborate on the topic you are discussing.

- These questions are more focused than open-ended questions.
- They help your partner understand what you are interested in hearing more about.
- They further communication because they help you gain more information.
- When you ask these kinds of questions, you demonstrate to your partner that you are interested and that you are listening.

**VI-D.
Listening
Skills:
Practice
Exercises**

Now I'd like you to practice using these listening skills by completing the exercises in Handout 5.3. Take 5 minutes to complete the exercise. Then we will go over it as a group and discuss a few people's responses.

Handout 5.3.

Complete exercise.

Let's see what a few of you wrote for each item on this exercise. There is no one right answer or type of answer. The idea here is to make certain that you understand how these communication skills are used.

Discuss answers as a group.

10 minutes.

Outline	Presenter's Comments	Activity
VI. **Assertive** **Communication**	*Assertive communication* is a constructive way of expressing feelings and opinions. Let's read through Handout 5.4 together. The first page defines assertive behavior and contrasts it with passive and aggressive behavior.	Handout 5.4.
	Next, please complete the exercises on this handout. When you are finished, we will discuss them.	Complete exercises. Discuss answers.
	Answers: Example #1: Aggressive Example #2: Passive Example #3: Assertive	5 minutes.
VII. **Giving and** **Receiving** **Constructive** **Feedback**	Giving and receiving constructive feedback is another important communication skill. One effective way to do this is with the I-message. I am going to introduce this skill to you by describing what it doesn't sound like. Please refer to Handout 5.5.	Handout 5.5. 8 minutes.
VII-A. **You-Messages**	How do you think you would feel if your partner spoke to you like this?	Read examples of you-messages.
	Answer to look for: Bad, talked down to, disrespected, and so on.	
	If you want to demonstrate to your partner that you respect and esteem him or her, try speaking with I-messages instead. Let's look at the examples on this handout.	Read examples.
VII-B. **I-Messages**	Why do you think I-messages would be a more effective way of communicating than you-messages?	Ask question.
	Answers to look for: 1. When you start your statement with "I," you are taking responsibility for the statement. 2. The I-message sounds less blameful and less negative than the you-message.	
	Please complete the practice exercises on Handout 5.5. Take about 5 minutes.	Complete exercises.
	Who would like to share their responses with the rest of us? Keep in mind that there are no correct answers, but make certain that you understand the components of the I-message.	Discuss answers. 10 minutes.

Outline	Presenter's Comments	Activity
VIII. Resolving Conflicts	Resolving conflict is a critical skill in marriage. Handout 5.6 outlines 12 steps for successfully managing conflict.	Handout 5.6.
	Let's read through the steps of the process together.	Read through steps.
	• What would happen if you used a process like this most of the time?	Ask discussion questions.
	• What are the greatest barriers to using a process like this?	10 minutes.
	Answers to expect: Time, impatience.	
	How do you think you will respond to these barriers?	Ask question.
IX. Managing Anger	Managing angry feelings—yours and your partner's—is another important skill that will help you build a successful marriage. Handout 5.7 details a few constructive responses to situations where you feel angry.	Handout 5.7.
	Let's look at each example on the handout.	Complete and discuss the practice exercises together.
	Now that we've talked about what anger is and how it is often an automatic response to a trigger, let's spend a few moments on how to interrupt the process of an angry reaction.	5 minutes.
	Suggest that participants take notes on Handout 5.8.	Handout 5.8.
IX-A. Time-Out	1. *Time-out* is a very effective technique for breaking the sequence of behavior that leads to a blow-up. It works best if it is discussed ahead of time and both people agree to use it. Here is how it works:	Present information. 10 minutes.
	Either person in an interaction can initiate time-out. One person makes the time-out gesture like a referee in a football game: a T-sign with his or her hands. The other person is obligated to return the gesture and stop talking.	
	This technique does not involve making any further statement, such as "I am getting upset." The only thing that might be said is "Time-out."	
	The T-sign is a signal that it is best to separate for awhile to cool off; an hour works best. It is important to return after the hour.	
IX-B. Make a Contract	2. *Make a time-out contract.* To emphasize your commitment to changing your anger behavior, you and your partner may even decide to write and sign a contact	

5.13

Outline	Presenter's Comments	Activity

outlining the details of your time-out agreement. This is especially helpful if anger has become a significant threat to the relationship.

IX-C.
Ask
Questions

3. *Ask questions.* If anger is a response to personal pain, it may make sense to ask the other person, "What's hurting?"

IX-D.
Positive
Statements

4. *Positive statements.* It may be helpful to memorize a few positive statements to say to yourself when your anger is being triggered. These statements can remind that you can choose your behavior instead of reacting in a knee-jerk manner. For example:

- I can take care of my own needs.
- His needs are just as important as mine.
- I am able to make good choices.

IX-E.
Prepared
Response

5. *Be prepared with a response.* Here are a few statements and questions that will help deescalate anger. Commit one or two to memory and use them when a situation is becoming heated:

- What's bothering me is. . . .
- And what I think I'd like is. . . .
- What would you suggest we do about this?
- If this continues like this, I'll have to do *X* to take care of myself.
- What do you need now?
- So what you want is. . . .
- It feels like we're getting angry about this. I want to stop and cool down for a minute.

What other ideas do you have for deescalating anger? — Ask question.

X.
Business
Skills for
Marriages

Our last topic is a consideration how business skills can help you build a better marriage. Marriage is a partnership of people. Many of the skills that make businesses run successfully—planning, organizing, and setting goals—also can be applied to running your marriage successfully. — Handout 5.9.
10 minutes.

Please take a look at Handout 5.9.

Let's look at each item and think of examples of how it would apply to your marriage. — Present information.

- What is an example of how you might carry out each of these items? — Ask discussion questions.

Outline	*Presenter's Comments*	*Activity*

- How might each of the items have a positive effect on a marriage?

1. Create an overall vision of what you want your life to be like; consider all life areas (see list of words on the second page of the handout).
2. Develop a long-range strategy.
3. Set short-term and long-term goals.
4. Plan the steps that will help you accomplish your goals.
5. Organize projects.
6. Manage projects.
7. Manage people.
8. Evaluate progress and results at regular intervals.
9. Revise goals as needed.

After today's workshop, I encourage each of you to set aside time to work on this list.

I also want to point out the list of life areas on the third page of this handout. These will help you set goals in a variety of areas.

XI.
What's Next?
🕐

Handout 5.10 is the final exercise of today's workshop. Please take 10 minutes to complete it on your own. When you are finished, take 5 more minutes to discuss it with your partner, if he or she is here.

Who would like to share what you wrote?

Handout 5.10.

Complete and share.

If time is limited, suggest as postworkshop assignment.

2–8 minutes.

XII.
Conclusion

I hope you have enjoyed today's workshop. In the time remaining, I would be happy to answer any questions you may have.

Conclude the workshop.

Handout 5.1   12 Roadblocks to Effective Communication

1. Ordering, directing, and commanding

_____

2. Warning, admonishing, and threatening

_____

3. Moralizing, preaching, and imploring

_____

4. Advising and giving suggestions or solutions

_____

5. Persuading with logic, lecturing, and arguing

_____

6. Judging, criticizing, disagreeing, and blaming

_____

7. Praising, agreeing, evaluating positively, and buttering up

_____

8. Name calling, ridiculing, and shaming

_____

9. Interpreting, analyzing, and diagnosing

_____

10. Reassuring, sympathizing, consoling, and supporting

_____

11. Probing, questioning, and interrogating

_____

12. Distracting, diverting, and kidding

_____

Source: Thomas Gordon, _Leader Effectiveness Training_ (New York: Bantam Doubleday Dell, 1986). Adapted and reprinted with permission.

Handout 5.2 Active Listening Practice Exercises

Write an *active listening* response to each of the following statements.

1. Your partner says, "I had the worst day! Two of my staff members called in sick and I had to present the new catalog to our client by myself. Then I couldn't get my car started when it was finally time to come home. And I almost got rear-ended on the freeway!"

   I would say: _____

   _____

   _____

2. You come home earlier than usual and find your husband busily cleaning up the mess he and your son have made with a school project. They seem annoyed that you are home.

   I would say: _____

   _____

   _____

3. "I don't know about that vacation. Now I'm having second thoughts about it. It's way more than we can afford. How will we ever be able to get away and do something fun?"

   I would say: _____

   _____

   _____

1. Open-Ended Questions

Ask open-ended questions to encourage your partner to talk to you and share his or her feelings.

Definition: Open-ended questions cannot be answered "yes" or "no." They are phrased to encourage the other person to give a broad response to your question.

Examples: "How do you feel about what she said?"

"Tell me all about your day today."

"What do you think about the new house?"

Other benefits of asking open-ended questions:

_____

_____

2. Summary Statements

Summarize what you hear your partner saying. A summary statement enhances your partner's self-esteem by showing that you were listening carefully.

Definition: A statement that summarizes the facts you gathered.

Examples: "So you're saying you want to go to Cedar Falls before you visit your brother. Then you want to come home."

"You're saying that you tried your best, but it was beyond your control."

Other benefits of making summary statements:

_____

_____

3. Neutral Questions and Phrases

Definition: Questions that encourage your partner to elaborate on some aspect of the topic.

Examples: "Give me some more reasons why we should buy the car now rather than in January."

"Tell me more about why you want to take this job."

Other benefits of neutral questions and phrases:

_____

_____

Practice Exercises

Directions: Choose a listening skill for each situation. Write an example of what you could say to the other person to validate his or her feelings and encourage further expression of emotion.

1. Your partner comes home from an important business trip. He is very quiet. When you ask him how the trip went, he shrugs his shoulders and says, "Okay."

   Which listening skill
   would work best here? _____

   I would say: _____

   _____

2. "I really wish we didn't have to go to that awful wedding next weekend. I know I have to, but I wish I could get out of it somehow. I don't like your cousin, I feel uncomfortable with her family, and I resent having to spend money on clothes and travel—not to mention a gift!"

   Which listening skill
   would work best here? _____

   I would say: _____

   _____

3. "I wish I could just stay in bed this morning," your husband says.

   Which listening skill
   would work best here? _____

   I would say: _____

   _____

4. You are 20 minutes late to pick up your partner. There was no way you could let him know you were going to be late. When you arrive, he opens the car door and glares at you. He growls, "I thought we agreed that you'd be on time for once!"

   Which listening skill
   would work best here? _____

   I would say: _____

   _____

5. Your wife wants to buy a used Ford Taurus and you think you should buy a new model. She says, "It makes me so nervous to take out such a big loan! And what if we don't like the Taurus? Besides, my father would never let me hear the end of it."

   Which listening skill
   would work best here? _____

   I would say: _____

   _____

Handout 5.4   Assertive Communication

Assertive behavior enables you to:

- Act in your own best interests
- Stand up for yourself without becoming anxious
- Express your honest feelings
- Assert your personal rights, without denying the rights of others

Assertive behavior is:

- Self-expressive
- Honest
- Direct
- Self-enhancing
- Not harmful to others
- Appropriate to the person and situation rather than universal
- Socially responsible
- A combination of learned skills, not an inborn trait

Assertive behavior includes both *what* you say and *how* you say it.

Assertive, Aggressive, or Passive?

Read each of the following conversations and decide whether each illustrates aggressive, passive, or assertive behavior.

Example #1

ELLEN: Listen, I've got a big problem with what you did. I've had it with these stupid mistakes in the checkbook. You either stop screwing up, or we're finished!

JACK: Give me a break, Ellen. You know it wasn't my fault.

ELLEN: Yeah, right! All I ever hear from you is excuses!

JACK: Those aren't excuses, Ellen. They're facts.

ELLEN: When are you going to do it the way I told you to do it?

Ellen's behavior is: _____

Example #2

ELLEN: Jack, I wish you'd be more careful with the checkbook.

JACK: I told you, Ellen, it wasn't my fault.

ELLEN: Oh, I'm sorry. You're right.

Ellen's behavior is: _____

Example #3

ELLEN: Jack, these mistakes created a big problem for me. I ended up bouncing a check and now I feel very embarrassed.

JACK: I told you, Ellen, it wasn't my fault.

ELLEN: I know you've had some problems, Jack. But I have to ask you to double-check your deposits in the future, and make sure you list all of your withdrawals. Will you agree to do that?

JACK: Sure, I think I can agree to that.

ELLEN: Thanks, Jack. I hope this solves the problem.

Ellen's behavior is: _____

Source: Robert Alberti and Michael Emmons, *Your Perfect Right* (Atascadero, CA: Impact, 1995).

Handout 5.5   You-Messages, I-Messages

You-Messages

Examples: You need to come home by 5 P.M. tomorrow.

You shouldn't do that.

You should call me from the airport and tell me when you'll be home.

You are rude to my friends.

Here is what you ought to do.

Why they damage relationships:

_____

_____

I-Messages

Components: Behavior + feelings + effects

Examples: When I'm not kept informed about what's going on, I get worried and start imagining that you're having problems that are not getting solved.

When you don't call from the airport, I feel disappointed that I can't have a nice dinner ready for you when you get home.

When I heard that you'd planned a weekend up north, I was confused about why you hadn't asked me first, so I could be sure to get the time off.

Why they are more effective than you-messages:

_____

_____

Practice Exercises

Convert these you-messages to I-messages and see how much more positive they sound:

1. You need to come home by 5 P.M. tomorrow.

I-message: _____

_____

2. You are rude to my friends.

I-message: _____

_____

3. Here is what you ought to do.

I-message: _____

_____

4. You should have chosen something more appropriate to wear.

I-message: _____

_____

Handout 5.6   Managing Conflict

1. Agree on the rules ahead of time.

2. Choose a time when you both feel calm.

3. Call a time-out if emotions begin to escalate. Set a time to return.

4. One person has the floor at a time. Set a timer if you wish.

5. Alternate the roles of speaker and listener as you each present your point of view.

   Speaker: State how you see the problem.

   Focus on the problem, not the person.

   Use I-messages.

   Listener: Ask questions to clarify and further your understanding.

   Summarize the issues as you understand them.

   Listen and avoid judging what the speaker says.

6. Each person states his or her point of view.

7. When both partners have stated their points of view, come to an agreement on what the problems are.

8. Brainstorm solutions.

9. State what action each of you would be willing to take.

10. Agree on a solution that fits both of your needs.

11. Agree on an action plan.

12. Follow through and take action.

Handout 5.7   A Better Response

Many of our angry responses occur because we simply don't take the time to think ahead and plan an alternative. Take a moment to consider these three constructive alternatives to anger.

1. Set Limits

Example: You are angry that your husband brought your car home dirty. He had taken several friends to a football game and out for a snack, and the car is full of trash and needs washing inside and out. You feel yourself about to blow up.

Sample response: (A) Acknowledge to yourself that your anger is your response. (B) Set limits. State your requests or demands clearly.

You could say to your husband: "I am very disappointed in the way the car looks. It is not acceptable for you to return it to me in this condition. I want you to get it cleaned right now. In the future, I will remind you of my expectations before I allow you to borrow my car."

Try another example: Last week, your wife borrowed a tape recorder from your office for a presentation. You told her that you needed it back no later than yesterday, but she still hasn't returned it. You call her at work to remind her to bring it home.

What could you say to your wife?

A. _____

B. _____

2. Don't Wait for Your Partner to Meet Your Needs

Example: You are angry that your husband hasn't mowed the lawn in two weeks. You are starting to be embarrassed by how the house looks. Your husband doesn't seem to be too concerned about it, but he is too busy at work to do much at home.

Sample response: (A) Acknowledge to yourself that your anger is your response. (B) Get your needs met some other way.

You could say to your husband: "I am embarrassed by the way the lawn looks. I understand that you don't have time to mow it. I'm going to hire the teenage boy across the street to take care of it for us. That way it won't bother me, and I won't have to feel angry at you."

Try another example: You need to buy a baby gift for a coworker. You were going to get it yourself, but your wife insisted that she has the time and has something special in mind. That was a month ago. The coworker is coming back to work soon and you feel embarrassed that you haven't sent a gift yet.

What could you say to your wife?

A. _____

B. _____

3. Be Assertive

Example: You told your wife at the beginning of the summer that you wanted to visit your parents one weekend. She agreed that it was a good idea, but whenever you ask her to choose a date, she is always too busy. You feel angry, because your parents won't be around forever. Meanwhile, it's almost August.

Sample response: (A) Acknowledge to yourself that your anger is your response. (B) Negotiate assertively.

You could say to your wife: "I am going to visit my parents next weekend. I want to get the visit in before the summer is over and I hope you'll be able to come along with me. Don't you agree that it's important?"

Try another example: You want to have your front door replaced before this winter. It's leaky and wastes lots of energy. You've brought it up to your husband before, and he seems to agree that it needs to be done. Your concern is that it will cost a few thousand dollars. In the past, a situation like this would have turned into an argument.

What could you say to your husband?

A. _____

B. _____

Handout 5.8　Five Ways to Interrupt Anger

The following five techniques may be helpful in stopping the spiral of anger.

1. Time out

   _____

   _____

2. Make a contract

   _____

   _____

3. Ask questions

   _____

   _____

4. Positive statements

   _____

   _____

5. Be prepared with a response

   _____

   _____

Handout 5.9   Business Skills/Marriage Skills

1. Create an overall vision of what you want your life to be like; consider all life areas (see end of handout).

    _____

    _____

    _____

2. Develop a long-range strategy.

    _____

    _____

    _____

3. Set short-term and long-term goals.

    _____

    _____

    _____

4. Plan the steps that will help you accomplish your goals.

    _____

    _____

    _____

5. Organize projects.

    _____

    _____

    _____

6. Manage projects.

    _____

    _____

    _____

7. Manage people.

_____

_____

_____

8. Evaluate progress and results at regular intervals.

_____

_____

_____

9. Revise goals as needed.

_____

_____

_____

Life Areas

Adventure	Home
Business	Income
Career	Knowledge
Church	Money
Clubs	Net worth
Communication	Politics
Community	Possessions
Contribution	Professional
Emotional	Reading
Exploring	Relationships
Family	Service
Fantasy	Spiritual
Fun	Study
Health	Travel
Hobbies	Work

Handout 5.10   What's Next?

1. What are the five most important things you have learned today about how to strengthen your marriage?

   - _____

   - _____

   - _____

   - _____

   - _____

2. What five actions do you plan to take to build your marriage?

   - _____

   - _____

   - _____

   - _____

   - _____

3. What five actions will you ask your partner to take?

   - _____

   - _____

   - _____

   - _____

   - _____

4. What are three things you want to know more about?

   - _____

   - _____

   - _____

5. How will you learn about them?

   - _____

   - _____

   - _____

Chapter 6

The Marriage Checkup

Presentation Synopsis

This workshop is designed for couples who have been married one year or longer. It is based on recent marital research conducted by Judith Wallerstein and John Gottman. The workshop provides a process for couples to compare their relationship to the behaviors outlined by these researchers. You may wish to combine the content from other workshop outlines to suit the needs of specific groups.

Workshop suggestions.   The following are three suggestions for presenting this information.

1. Present the information as a lecture. Distribute the handouts and walk the participants through the content. Suggest that they complete Handout 6.1 at home and offer them a private follow-up session with you to discuss the results.
2. Use this information to work with couples in your office. Ask them to complete Handout 6.1 at home *before* the session. Use their answers to each item as a framework for helping them determine how to strengthen their marriage.
3. Promote your practice by offering the marriage checkup with a free or low-cost session just before Valentine's Day. Present workshops in your community or offer free introductory sessions for couples.

This presentation is based, in part, on information drawn from the following books. I recommend that you review them as you prepare your presentation:

Gottman, John. *The Seven Principles for Making Marriage Work.* New York: Crown, 1999.

Gottman, John. *Why Marriages Succeed or Fail and How You Can Make Yours Last.* New York: Fireside Books, 1994.

Wallerstein, Judith, and Sandra Blakeslee. *The Good Marriage: How and Why Love Lasts.* New York: Warner Books, 1995.

Time Requirements

This presentation runs from ½ hour to 1½ hours, depending on the style of the presenter and the number of interactive activities used.

☽ **Clock symbol.**   This means that the information is included for a longer seminar or workshop. Omit these sections for a shorter presentation. If time is limited, another way to shorten your presentation is to share the information in lecture format. However, keep in mind that it is often harder to engage and maintain the audience's interest with a pure lecture style. Unless you are a particularly dynamic speaker, you will probably want to keep at least a few of the exercises to enliven the presentation.

Video illustrations.   As you go through the items on the checkup handout, you may wish to make it more interesting by incorporating a few short scenes from current or classic movies rented from your local video store. Consider including scenes from movies that explore relationships. Examples include *The Big Chill, Grand Canyon, The Four Seasons, On Golden Pond, The Godfather, One True Thing, Mrs. Doubtfire,* or others.

How to Use This Presentation

Possible Audiences

Adult education groups at churches and synagogues

PTO/PTA

Civic and professional organizations

Whom to Contact

Director of adult education programs

PTO/PTA president

Director of educational programs

Sample Text for Marketing Letter, Brochure, or Postcard

Most adults engage in long-term relationships, including marriage and other committed partnerships. Nearly everyone experiences difficulties in their marriage or committed relationship from time to time, but some people seem more prepared to anticipate these hard times and respond to them more skillfully than others. The skills that make a marriage last can be learned, and "The Marriage Checkup" workshop provides an introduction.

_____ is offering this educational and motivational seminar to your group as a community service. In this workshop, participants learn several skills that will help them build and strengthen their marriages and long-term partnerships, including communication, listening, and conflict management skills.

_____ is a licensed _____ in private practice in _____. S/he specializes in _____ and _____. Call _____ today to schedule your group's **free** workshop. (_____) _____-_____.

Sample Text for Press Release

_____ Presents "The Marriage Checkup"

_____ is presenting a **free** workshop on how to build a thriving marriage or long-term committed relationship. The workshop is scheduled for _____, from _____ to _____ at

_____. It is designed for people who have been in their marriage or relationship for one year or more and is limited to _____ participants. It is open to members of _____ and the public.

    According to _____, "A long-term lasting marriage or other committed relationship has certain characteristics that cause it to thrive. One of those characteristics is that the people in the relationship are skilled at communication and know how to manage conflict. In this workshop, we will explore a few of the skills that anyone can learn for a positive impact on their marriage."

    _____ is a licensed _____ in private practice in _____. S/he specializes in _____ and _____. For reservations, call _____ at (_____) _____-_____.

Exhibit 6.1   Presentation Outline

The Marriage Check-Up

Topic	*Time Estimate*
I. **Introduction**	2–10 minutes
A. Introduce yourself	
🕐 B. Ask group members to introduce themselves	
C. State workshop goals	
II. **Background Research**	
🕐 A. Wallerstein's work	5–30 minutes
🕐 B. Gottman's work	2–10 minutes
III. **Marriage Check-Up Handout**	10–40 minutes
🕐 Video examples	
IV. **Schedule Follow-up Sessions**	
V. **Conclusion**	
Approximate Total Time	**20–90 minutes**

The Marriage Checkup

Outline	Presenter's Comments	Activity
I-A. **Introduce Yourself**	My name is _____. I'm a licensed _____, with a _____. I specialize in working with _____. I became interested in how to help couples keep their marriages strong after working with many who came to me too late. I started noticing this ____ ago, when _____ _____ _____.	Refer to your bio on the first page of the handouts. 1 minute.
I-B. **Group Intro** ⏱	I'd like to start things off today by finding out a bit about each of you. Please introduce yourself and tell us what you would like to get out of this experience.	If the group is under 20 people, ask participants to introduce themselves. 10 minutes.
I-C. **Goals**	The purpose of today's workshop is to introduce a process for evaluating your marriage. It is designed for couples who have been married 1 year or longer and is based on recent marital research conducted by psychologists Judith Wallerstein and John Gottman.	State goals. 1 minute.
II. **Background Research**	The marriage checkup (Handout 6.1) is a questionnaire that outlines 15 points for evaluating your marriage. These points are derived from recent research completed by the two psychologists.	Handout 6.1.
II-A. **Wallerstein's Work**	The first research we'll look at was conducted by psychologist Judith Wallerstein in the early 1990s. She details her work in *The Good Marriage: How and Why Love Lasts,* which she coauthored with Sandra Blakeslee. Wallerstein studied 50 couples who had been married an average of 21 years. She wanted to learn why some marriages succeed while others fail. She wanted to know how the people in good marriages differ from those in bad ones. Wallerstein found that to have a successful marriage, couples must complete nine tasks during their lifetime. Based on her interviews with the 50 couples, she determined that couples whose marriages are unsuccessful failed to	5–30 minutes.

Outline	Presenter's Comments	Activity

complete these tasks. Those who stayed happily married accomplished all nine of them.

🕐 (Briefly describe Wallerstein's nine tasks. You may wish to use Handout 4.1 from the "Before the Wedding" presentation.)

Handout 4.1 from "Before the Wedding."

**II-B.
Gottman's
Work**

Several items on this questionnaire are based on the work of another psychologist, John Gottman, who has studied couples for 20 years. In his book *Why Marriages Succeed or Fail,* Gottman describes the behaviors which lead to long-term success and those which lead to divorce. His newer book, *The Seven Principles for Making Marriage Work,* presents much of the same information in a format designed for nonprofessionals.

Present information.

2–10 minutes.

🕐 (Briefly describe Gottman's skills for marriage success. You may wish to use Handouts 4.2 and 4.3 from the "Before the Wedding" presentation.)

Handouts 4.2 and 4.3 from "Before the Wedding."

**III.
Checkup
Handout**
🕐

Explain each item on the checkup exercise. If time allows, illustrate various points with scenes from popular videos.

Ask participants to complete the marriage checkup exercise at home. Suggest that they buy and read the Gottman and Wallerstein books.

Discuss items on Handout 6.1.

Illustrate with videos.

10–30 minutes.

Homework assignment.

**IV.
Schedule
Follow-up
Sessions**

(If you plan to offer private follow-up sessions with participants, make appointments now.)

Make follow-up appointments.

**V.
Conclusion**

I hope you have enjoyed today's workshop. In the time remaining, I would be happy to answer any questions you may have.

Conclude the workshop.

Handout 6.1   The Marriage Checkup

1. List your partner's positive qualities. Include as many things as you can think of.

_____   _____

_____   _____

_____   _____

_____   _____

_____   _____

2. My partner and I have invested ourselves fully in our marriage. While we have positive relationships with our parents, siblings, and other relatives, we are not overly involved with them.

Based on the signs listed below, where would you place your answer?

You

Not at all committed to the relationship   Completely committed to the relationship

1   2   3   4   5   6   7   8   9   10

Your Partner

Not at all committed to the relationship   Completely committed to the relationship

1   2   3   4   5   6   7   8   9   10

Signs that you have a healthy relationship with your family (neither too distant nor too involved):

	His	Hers
My partner and I mostly rely on each other to get our needs met.	_____	_____
Our families visit when invited.	_____	_____
Their visits are short but satisfying.	_____	_____
We speak by phone, but not too often.	_____	_____
They give advice when asked.	_____	_____

Signs that your family may be overly involved in your life:

	His	Hers
They visit too often.	_____	_____
They stay too long.	_____	_____
They telephone frequently.	_____	_____

	His	Hers
They give unsolicited advice.	_____	_____
They drop in unannounced.	_____	_____
We consult them for most decisions.	_____	_____

3. My partner and I have our own identity as a couple. There is a feeling of both togetherness and independence in our relationship.

Based on the signs listed below, where would you place your answer?

No sense of ourselves as a couple   Strong sense of ourselves as a couple
1   2   3   4   5   6   7   8   9   10

Signs that you have developed an identity as a couple:

____ We have our own rules for our relationship.

____ We have a shared view of our life together.

____ We feel loyal toward each other.

____ Our relationship has an identity; there is a "we."

____ We listen to each other.

____ We know each other's history.

____ We pay attention to each other's moods.

____ We pay attention to each other's body language.

____ We tell each other our thoughts and feelings.

____ We are willing to share with each other.

____ We allow each other a private space and don't intrude.

____ We respect each other as separate, autonomous people.

Signs that you have not fully developed your couple identity:

____ We have not agreed on rules for our relationship.

____ We have not developed a shared view of our life together.

____ We are sometimes disloyal toward each other.

____ We fail to listen to each other.

____ We know little about each other's history.

____ We ignore each other's moods.

____ We are unaware of each other's body language.

____ We hide our thoughts and feelings from each other.

_____ We avoid sharing things or time with each other.

_____ We sometimes intrude on each other's private space.

_____ Even though we live in the same house, it sometimes seems like we are living parallel lives.

4. (If you have children.) My partner and I have successfully made the transition from being a childless couple to being parents.

Based on the signs listed below, where would you place your answer?

You

Have not integrated children into the marriage   Have integrated children into the marriage

| 1 | 2 | 3 | 4 | 5 | 6 | 7 | 8 | 9 | 10 |

Your Partner

Has not integrated children into the marriage   Has integrated children into the marriage

| 1 | 2 | 3 | 4 | 5 | 6 | 7 | 8 | 9 | 10 |

Signs that you have successfully integrated children into your marriage:

_____ We accept that there are times when we have to sacrifice our own needs to meet the needs of our child.

_____ We strive to stay in touch with each other emotionally and nourish our relationship.

_____ We set aside time weekly for the two of us to spend time alone together.

Signs that you have not fully integrated children into your marriage:

_____ We resent the times when we must sacrifice our own needs to meet the needs of our child.

_____ We are probably too focused on our child.

_____ We have lost touch with each other emotionally and our relationship has suffered.

_____ We rarely set aside time for the two of us to spend time alone together.

5. Our relationship has been tested by life transitions and crises.

Marriage has been damaged by crises   Marriage has weathered crises

| 1 | 2 | 3 | 4 | 5 | 6 | 7 | 8 | 9 | 10 |

Signs that you have successfully navigated crises and transitions:

_____ We do not blame each other for the stress that comes with a crisis.

_____ We face difficult times as a team.

_____ It is important to us to support each other emotionally when times are difficult.

_____ We work hard to keep our perspective when there is a crisis.

_____ We seek outside support when we are in a crisis.

Signs that crises and transitions may harm your marriage:

____ One partner abandons the other emotionally.

____ One partner blames the other when there is a crisis.

____ One partner becomes angry when there is a crisis.

____ We become overwhelmed with worry and anxiety in a crisis.

____ We don't seek outside support when we are in crisis.

6. Our relationship is a place where anger, conflict, and differences may safely be expressed. It is okay for each of us to have and express our own views.

You

Make it difficult to express conflict   Make it safe to express conflict

| 1 | 2 | 3 | 4 | 5 | 6 | 7 | 8 | 9 | 10 |

Your Partner

Makes it difficult to express conflict   Makes it safe to express conflict

| 1 | 2 | 3 | 4 | 5 | 6 | 7 | 8 | 9 | 10 |

Signs that it is safe to express conflict:

____ Even though we have had serious differences, we have kept our conflicts from causing damage to our relationship.

____ We agree to disagree.

____ We respect the other person's right to stand his or her ground.

____ Anger is uncomfortable, but it is part of life.

____ We have rules about containing conflict. We know that there are limits to what the other will do when angry.

Signs that it is not safe to express conflict:

____ Our conflicts have damaged our relationship.

____ We disagree about many things but never talk about it.

____ We both try to bully the other into agreeing with our point of view.

____ Anger is so uncomfortable that it must be avoided.

____ There are no limits to what we will do when angry.

7. We have a satisfying sexual relationship. We take care to protect it from the demands of work and family.

Signs of a satisfying sexual relationship:

____ We sometimes have different levels of desire, but we accommodate each other's changing needs.

_____ We talk candidly about our changing desires and feelings.

_____ We make time for our sexual relationship.

_____ We protect our privacy and guard our sexual relationship.

Signs that your sexual relationship is less than satisfying:

_____ We find it difficult to talk about sex.

_____ Sex is like a battlefield for us.

_____ We never have time for sex.

_____ Having children has interfered with our sex life.

8. We share laughter and fun times, and keep our mutual interests alive.

Signs that your marriage is fun:

_____ We have fun together.

_____ We make each other laugh.

_____ We find each other interesting.

_____ We enjoy the time we spend together.

_____ We each have our own interests that we pursue without our partner.

_____ We enjoy having new experiences.

Signs that your marriage is in danger of becoming stale:

_____ We don't have much fun together.

_____ We don't laugh much when we are together.

_____ We find each other boring.

_____ We avoid spending time together.

_____ We have no common interests.

_____ We avoid new experiences.

9. We comfort and encourage each other. We view our relationship as a safe place where we can be ourselves and be vulnerable.

Signs that you comfort and encourage each other:

_____ It is okay to be needy and vulnerable in our marriage.

_____ We fill up each other's emotional reserves.

_____ We understand each other.

_____ We encourage each other.

_____ We pay attention to each other's moods and respond when the other seems needy.

_____ When I'm worried, my partner reassures me.

Signs that your relationship may not be a safe and comforting place:

_____ It is not safe to let my guard down with my partner.

_____ It is not safe to be needy and vulnerable in our marriage.

_____ We deplete each other's emotional reserves.

_____ We ignore each other's moods.

_____ When I'm worried about something, the last person I want to tell is my partner.

_____ I feel worse about myself when I am with my partner.

10. We maintain a romantic and idealistic view of our relationship, while at the same time facing the reality that we are growing older and will never be young again.

Signs that you have maintained the romance of your relationship:

_____ I have good memories of when we fell in love.

_____ I am glad to be growing older with my partner.

Signs that you have lost some of the romance of your relationship:

_____ I have a hard time remembering the days when we fell in love.

_____ Seeing my partner grow older makes me feel bad because it reminds me that I am growing older.

11. The positive moments in our marriage far outnumber the negative moments.

Examples of positive moments:

_____ We show that we are interested in each other.

_____ We show each other affection.

_____ We express appreciation to each other.

_____ We apologize for hurtful things we may have said or done.

_____ We show each other empathy.

_____ We are polite to each other.

_____ Each of us knows that the other has our best interests at heart.

Examples of negative moments:

_____ Our discussions often result in frustration.

_____ We often pick on each other.

_____ Our discussions often lead to a dead end.

____ Many of our conversations turn into arguments.

____ We speak and act disrespectfully to each other.

____ We call each other names.

____ We are physically violent.

____ We mimic each other when we are angry.

12. We manage conflict productively and keep it from getting out of control.

Examples of managing conflict productively:

____ We call a time-out when our emotions escalate.

____ We set a time limit when we are in conflict.

____ We know how to calm ourselves down.

____ We speak and listen nondefensively.

____ We take care to validate the other person's point of view, even when we disagree with it.

Examples of allowing conflict to become damaging:

____ We criticize each other.

____ We verbally attack each other.

____ We blame each other.

____ We insult each other.

____ We treat each other disrespectfully.

____ We call each other names.

____ We make excuses for our behavior.

____ We deny responsibility for our actions.

____ We get so angry that we storm out of the room or emotionally withdraw.

Check If Yes

13. My partner uses drugs or alcohol in a way that creates problems.   _____

14. My partner manages money in a way that creates problems.   _____

15. My partner does not take proper care of his or her health. I am
concerned about whether he or she will grow old with me.   _____

Sources: John Gottman, *Why Marriages Succeed or Fail and How You Can Make Yours Last* (New York: Fireside Books, 1994); Judith Wallerstein and Sandra Blakeslee, *The Good Marriage: How and Why Love Lasts* (New York: Warner Books, 1995).

Chapter 7

Recovering from
Infidelity

Presentation Synopsis

This workshop focuses on what infidelity is, how to recognize it, and why it happens. Other topics include the consequences of infidelity, how to recover, and how to prevent it. This informative and interactive workshop includes mini-lectures, written exercises, group discussion, and video examples.

This presentation is based, in part, on information found in the following books. You may wish to review them as you prepare your presentation:

Pittman, Frank. *Private Lies: Infidelity and the Betrayal of Intimacy.* New York: W. W. Norton, 1989.

Staheli, Lana. *Affair-Proof Your Marriage: Understanding, Preventing and Surviving an Affair.* New York: HarperCollins, 1995.

Subotnik, Rona, and Gloria Harris. *Surviving Infidelity: Making Decisions, Recovering from the Pain.* Holbrook, MA: Adams, 1994.

Vaughan, Peggy. *The Monogamy Myth.* New York: Newmarket Press, 1989.

Time Requirements

This presentation runs from 1 hour to 1½ hours, depending on the style of the presenter and the number of interactive activities used.

🕐 **Clock symbol.**   This means that the information is included for a longer seminar or workshop. Omit these sections for a shorter presentation. If time is limited, another way to shorten your presentation is to share the information in lecture format. However, keep in mind that it is often harder to engage and maintain the audience's interest with a pure lecture style. Unless you are a particularly dynamic speaker, you will probably want to keep at least a few of the exercises to enliven the presentation.

How to Use This Presentation

Possible Audiences	Whom to Contact
Adult education groups at churches and synagogues	Director of adult education programs
PTO/PTA	PTO/PTA president
Women's civic and professional organizations	Director of educational programs

Sample Text for Marketing Letter, Brochure, or Postcard

_____ is offering a workshop titled "Recovering from Infidelity" to your group as a community service. This informative session focuses on what infidelity is, how to recognize it, and why it happens. Other topics include the consequences of infidelity, how to recover, and how to prevent it. This educational and interactive workshop includes mini-lectures, written exercises, group discussion, and video examples.

_____ is a licensed _____ in private practice in _____. S/he specializes in _____ and _____. Call _____ today to schedule your group's **free** workshop. (_____) _____-_____.

Sample Text for Press Release

_____ Presents "Recovering from Infidelity" Session

_____ is presenting a **free** workshop on how to recover from an extramarital affair. The workshop is scheduled for _____, from _____ to _____. It is limited to ____ participants and is open to the public.

According to _____, "It is estimated that 60 percent of men and 40 percent of women today will have an extramarital affair during their marriage. Even though it is devastating, marriages can recover. And there are many ways couples can prevent it from happening to them. This educational and interactive workshop focuses on what infidelity is, how to recognize it, and why it happens. We will also look at the consequences of infidelity, how to recover, and how to prevent it."

_____ is a licensed _____ in private practice in _____. S/he specializes in _____ and _____. For reservations, call _____ at (_____) _____-_____.

Exhibit 7.1   Presentation Outline

Recovering from Infidelity

Topic	*Time Estimate*
1. Introduction	2–12 minutes
A. Introduce yourself	
🕐 B. Ask group members to introduce themselves	
C. State workshop goals	
II. Definition of Infidelity	1 minute
III. Forms of Infidelity	1 minute
IV. Why Affairs Happen	5 minutes
🕐 A. Relationship factors (video examples)	4 minutes
B. Social reasons for infidelity	5–10 minutes
V. Signs of Infidelity	10–15 minutes
🕐	
VI. Infidelity Facts	10–20 minutes
🕐	
VII. Consequences of Infidelity	10 minutes
A. Common reactions to infidelity	
B. Other consequences	
VIII. Recovery Strategies	10–15 minutes
A. If you were unfaithful	
🕐 B. If your partner was unfaithful	
IX. Prevention Steps	10–15 minutes
🕐	
X. Conclusion	
Approximate Total Time	**68–108 minutes**

Recovering from Infidelity

Outline	Presenter's Comments	Activity
I-A. **Introduce Yourself**	My name is _____. I'm a licensed _____, with a _____. I specialize in working with _____. As a therapist, I have worked with many individuals and couples whose marriages have been affected by infidelity. As I have learned more about it, I have discovered that infidelity is more common than most people realize. In fact, it is estimated that 60 percent of men and 40 percent of women today will have an extramarital affair during their marriage. I decided to learn as much as I could about it so I could help my clients prevent it, or recover from it when it has already happened.	Refer to your bio on the first page of the handouts. 1 minute.
I-B. **Group Intro** ⏱	Before we begin the workshop, I'd like to learn something about each of you. Let's go around the room and each person introduce him- or herself. If there is something special you would like to learn from today's workshop, go ahead and say what that is. I'll do my best to address it.	If the group is under 20 people, ask participants to introduce themselves. 10 minutes.
I-C. **Goals**	This workshop explores the forces that lead to infidelity and what must happen for couples to heal.	State goals. 1 minute.
II. **Definition of Infidelity**	In his book *Private Lies,* author Frank Pittman defines infidelity as the betrayal of a relationship. It is a breach of trust and the breaking of the agreement that a couple will be sexually exclusive. In describing how infidelity destroys marriages, Pittman says that "Infidelity may not be the worst thing that one marriage partner can do to another, but it may be the most confusing and disorienting and therefore the most likely to destroy the marriage—not necessarily because of the sex, but because of the secrecy and the lies" (page 22). Lying and then hiding the lie amount to a "deliberate effort to disorient your partner"—and that is devastating. As devastating as infidelity may be, healing is possible and marriages can be saved.	Mini-lecture. 1 minute.

Outline	Presenter's Comments	Activity
III. **Forms of** **Infidelity**	Infidelity takes many forms. Some people have serial affairs—a series of one-night stands or short affairs. • These affairs involve very little emotional investment and may be rationalized as harmless. • There is always the danger of contracting a sexually transmitted disease. • And when such behavior goes on for several years, and finally is discovered, it is difficult to heal the years of deceit. Other affairs are single events and also involve little emotional investment. Sometimes affairs last longer and become more serious. These affairs may be very romantic and sexual. Sometimes they grow into more serious relationships that may last for years.	1 minute.
IV. **Why Affairs** **Happen**	Infidelity happens for many reasons. You may want to note these on Handout 7.1. Pittman says that "most of the reasons have to do with the ego state of the person having the affair rather than person against whom the infidelity is being committed" (page 39). Here are a few of the common explanations for why affairs happen:	Handout 7.1. Mini-lecture. 5 minutes.
IV-A. **Relationship** **Factors**	1. An affair may be a response to the anxiety caused by a life transition, such as a death, moving to a new town, job change, or midlife crisis. 2. One partner may have grown bored with the other and seeks excitement in someone new who seems to provide the missing spark.	
⊘	In his movie *Husbands and Wives*, Woody Allen provides several examples of people who seek escape from their marriages at midlife by having affairs. • In one scene, Woody Allen's character becomes attracted to a pretty 20-year-old played by Juliette Lewis. • In another scene, Sidney Pollack's character leaves his wife and has a relationship with a young woman. 3. Stressful times in the family life cycle may lead some to seek escape in an affair. Examples include taking care of aging parents, raising teenagers, and becoming parents.	If time allows, show two video scenes. 4 minutes.

Outline	Presenter's Comments	Activity

4. Some seek outside relationships when they begin to feel dissatisfied because their expectations of the marriage have not been fulfilled.

5. Another reason is that one's partner may be emotionally unavailable because of illness.

6. Other people begin affairs because they are seeking more affection than their partner is willing to provide.

7. Other people are seeking professional or social advancement.

8. Still others have affairs because they want more sex or more variety in sex.

IV-B.
Social
Reasons for
Infidelity

In *The Monogamy Myth,* author Peggy Vaughan argues that the reasons for affairs most often lie outside of individual relationships. She says that "affairs happen in so many marriages that it's unreasonable to think they're due solely to factors within each marriage" (page 25).

5 minutes.

Vaughan says that there are several powerful factors in our society that may explain why infidelity is so common:

1. There is a great deal of dishonesty in our society about all matters relating to sex. We are conditioned not to talk about it or to question each other about it.

2. We are conditioned not to trust people of the opposite gender.

3. We have restrictive role expectations for husbands and wives. Affairs provide a way to relate to people in more exciting and playful ways, which isn't allowed in our marriages.

4. In advertising, women are often portrayed as one-dimensional sex objects. Models and actresses are almost exclusively beautiful and perfect, causing most women to feel ugly or plain in comparison. Vaughan says that many women have affairs to validate their attractiveness and therefore feel reassured about their worth.

5. Our society leads us to expect a fairy-tale version of marriage. When our marriage doesn't live up to this expectation, we continue to look for it outside of our marriage.

What is your reaction to these ideas?

What other reasons can you think of?

Lead discussion.

5 minutes.

7.7

Outline	Presenter's Comments	Activity
V. **Signs of Infidelity** 🕐	How can you tell if your partner is having an affair? Handout 7.2 lists some signs that may point to infidelity. Let's discuss each of these and see if you have any to add.	Handout 7.2. Present information. 10 minutes. Ask for additional ideas & reactions. 5 minutes.
VI. **Infidelity Facts** 🕐	Handout 7.3 lists several facts about infidelity. Let's discuss each of these and see what your reaction is to each one. *The Monogamy Myth* by Peggy Vaughan contains the following statistics: 60 percent of men and 40 percent of women will have an extramarital affair. The Kinsey Report in the 1940s and 1950s showed that by age 40, 50 percent of the men had had an extramarital affair. The Kinsey Report showed that by age 40, 26 percent of the women had had an extramarital affair. The Hite Report on Male Sexuality of 1980 found that 72 percent of men married 2 years or more had had an extramarital affair. Shere Hite's 1987 survey of women found that 70 percent of women married 5 years or more had had an extramarital affair. People who have affairs are more likely to divorce. 80 percent of those who divorce as the result of an affair later regret their decision. Approximately 15 percent of women and 25 percent of men have more than 4 affairs during their married lives. Fewer than 10 percent of people having affairs divorce their spouse and marry their lover. 75 percent of these marriages end in divorce. When a marriage survives an affair, it takes between 1 and 3 years to recover. • What surprises you? • Are the numbers higher or lower than you expected?	Handout 7.3. Present information. 10 minutes. Ask for reactions. 10 minutes.
VII. **Consequences of Infidelity**	Let's discuss the emotional impact and other consequences of infidelity. Please take a look at Handout 7.4.	Handout 7.4.

Outline	Presenter's Comments	Activity
VII-A. Common Reactions to Infidelity	Common emotional reactions to infidelity include:	Present information. 10 minutes.
	1. First, a physical reaction like feeling like you have been punched in the stomach.	
	2. Many people have the classic reactions to loss, identified by Dr. Elisabeth Kübler-Ross. These include:	
	• Denial (How could this be happening to me?) • Anger (I could kill him! How could he do this?) • Bargaining (Maybe if I could be more loving, this will all go away.) • Depression (loss of appetite, confusion, tearfulness, and self-neglect) • Acceptance (first intellectual, then emotional)	
	Other common reactions include:	
	3. Blaming yourself (I wasn't sexy enough, didn't pay enough attention, not smart enough, etc.).	
	4. Blaming your partner (I can't believe anything he says.).	
	5. Blaming the relationship (We were too different, we were wrong for each other, we were too young, etc.).	
	6. Blaming the lover (It's all her fault, if it weren't for her); it is easy to transfer anger from one's spouse to one's lover.	
VII-B. Other Consequences	In addition to the emotional impact of infidelity, there may also be other consequences: sexually transmitted diseases, pregnancy, problems at work, and loss of relationships.	
VIII. Recovery Strategies	Even though infidelity has a devastating impact on a marriage, many marriages do survive. Let's look at what it takes for a relationship to recover. You may wish to take notes on Handout 7.5.	Handout 7.5. Present information. 10 minutes.
VIII-A. If You Were Unfaithful	If *you* had the affair and want to save your marriage:	
	1. Stop the affair and tell the truth about it.	
	2. Make the choice to practice fidelity.	
	3. Understand your partner's need to ask questions and understand what happened.	
	4. Spend plenty of time with your family.	
	5. Find a therapist and explore what has happened in your marriage.	

Outline	Presenter's Comments	Activity

6. Expect to reassure your partner of your commitment to the marriage.

7. Listen carefully to your partner and accept his or her feelings and thoughts.

8. When something you did is really bothering you, make a list of the steps you could take to make it right. Develop a plan to clean up the mess. Start with one small step today.

9. Admit you were wrong. Write a letter to the person involved in the situation and admit everything. Let it all out.

10. Make amends. Identify what it would take for you to feel absolved of guilt. Then, do it.

**VIII-B.
If Your
Partner Was
Unfaithful**

If *your partner* had the affair and you want to save your marriage:

1. Acknowledge your anger and express it productively.

2. Be aware of distorted thoughts that may increase your anger.

3. Watch out for negative beliefs that may make repairing your relationship more difficult.

4. Find a way to explore and express your feelings. Write in a journal or see a therapist.

5. Explore the pros and cons of preserving your marriage.

6. Establish a safe environment where you can learn about what happened.

7. When you are ready, create a ritual for letting go of the anger and forgiving.

What other ideas would you like to add to these lists?

Ask for more ideas.

5 minutes.

**IX.
Prevention
Steps**

Finally, what are some things you can do to protect your marriage from becoming an infidelity statistic? I'd like to hear your ideas on this subject. Let's list them on the easel. You may wish to make a list of these ideas on Handout 7.6.

Handout 7.6.

List group's ideas on easel.

10–15 minutes.

Outline	Presenter's Comments	Activity

🕐

When the group is finished listing ideas, add any from the following list that have not already been suggested:

1. Pay attention to your partner. Be aware of his or her needs and do your best to meet them.

2. Think about how you behaved when you were trying to win your partner over. Do the same things now.

3. Make sex fun.

4. Look for opportunities to talk and listen.

5. Be thoughtful and romantic. Send cards, flowers, or gifts.

6. Avoid high-risk situations. Discuss these with your partner and ask him or her to do the same.

7. Be polite to your partner.

8. Say nice things about your partner, in public and in private.

9. Spend regular private time together.

10. Greet your partner when he or she comes home.

11. Be enthusiastic and friendly. Show that you are glad to see your partner.

12. Remind yourself of your values. Commit to living in accordance with what you believe is right.

13. Accept that you are responsible for your own well-being.

14. Be proactive about nurturing your marriage. This relationship is your most important investment; give it the time and creativity it deserves.

15. Look for ways to express appreciation and respect. Think of ways to enhance your partner's self-esteem.

Activity column:
Encourage participants to be specific and give examples.

If time is limited, you may present these points as a lecture.

X. Conclusion

I hope you have enjoyed today's workshop. In the time remaining, I would be happy to answer any questions you may have.

Conclude the workshop.

Handout 7.1 Reasons for Infidelity

Factors in relationships:

1. _____

2. _____

3. _____

4. _____

5. _____

6. _____

7. _____

8. _____

9. _____

Factors in society:

1. _____

2. _____

3. _____

4. _____

5. _____

Handout 7.2   Signs of Infidelity

The following signs may point to infidelity by your partner:

1. Has recently lost weight.

2. Has changed hair color or style.

3. Wears a different style of underwear.

4. Pays more attention to clothing and appearance.

5. Changes brand of soap or shampoo.

6. Uses breath mints.

7. Stops wearing his or her wedding band.

8. Wears more jewelry.

9. Buys a sports car.

10. Changes position of car's passenger seat.

11. Has repeatedly called one number on the cellular phone bill.

12. Doesn't leave a number where he or she can be reached.

13. Gives vague answers about where he or she will be.

14. Has sudden work obligations that prevent attendance at family events.

15. Goes to more conferences than in the past.

16. Has more client dinners than in the past.

17. Has an extra key on his or her key ring.

18. Has restaurant matchbooks in his or her pocket.

19. Has lipstick or makeup on shirt.

20. Makes frequent excuses to go out alone.

21. Goes for more workouts at the gym.

22. Smells like he or she just took a shower.

23. Seems emotionally distant or preoccupied.

24. Seems less interested in family activities.

25. Changes sexual behavior (wants more or less).

26. You have a gut feeling that something is wrong.

Handout 7.3 Infidelity Facts

_____ of men and _____ of women will have an extramarital affair.

The Kinsey Report in the 1940s and 1950s showed that by age 40, _____

_____.

The Kinsey Report showed that by age 40, _____

_____.

The Hite Report on Male Sexuality of 1980 found that _____

_____.

Shere Hite's 1987 survey of women found that _____

_____.

People who have affairs are more likely to _____

_____.

80 percent of those who divorce as the result of an affair later _____

_____.

Approximately _____ of women and _____ of men have more than four affairs during their married lives.

Fewer than _____ of people having affairs divorce their spouse and marry their lover. _____ of these marriages end in divorce.

When a marriage survives an affair, it takes _____ years to recover.

Source: Peggy Vaughan, _The Monogamy Myth_. Copyright © 1989, 1998 by Peggy Vaughan. Reprinted with the permission of Newmarket Press, New York.

Handout 7.4 Infidelity: The Emotional Impact and Other Consequences

Common reactions to infidelity:

1. _____

2. _____

    • _____

    • _____

    • _____

    • _____

    • _____

3. _____

4. _____

5. _____

6. _____

Other consequences:

7. _____

8. _____

9. _____

10. _____

7.15

Handout 7.5   How to Recover from Infidelity

If you had the affair and want to save your marriage:

1. _____

2. _____

3. _____

4. _____

5. _____

6. _____

7. _____

8. _____

If your partner had the affair and you want to save your marriage:

1. _____

2. _____

3. _____

4. _____

5. _____

6. _____

Handout 7.6   How to Prevent Infidelity

1. _____
2. _____
3. _____
4. _____
5. _____
6. _____
7. _____
8. _____
9. _____
10. _____
11. _____
12. _____
13. _____
14. _____
15. _____

Chapter 8

Single-Parent
Survival Skills

Presentation Synopsis

This presentation explores ways that single parents can seek and find support for their very challenging situations. Through written exercises and group discussions, you will help your audience explore the emotional overload that many single parents experience, ways to enhance the process of recovering from loss, and how to listen to your children with empathy. You will also discuss a list of 28 strategies that will help single parents survive and even thrive during the coming years.

This workshop contains references to information presented in the following books. You may wish to review them as you prepare your presentation:

Alberti, Robert, and Michael Emmons. *Your Perfect Right,* 7th ed. Atascadero, CA: Impact, 1995.

Ames, Louise Bates, Frances L. Ilg, and Sidney M. Baker. *Your Ten- to Fourteen-Year-Old.* New York: Dell Trade Paperbacks, 1988. (This book is part of the Gesell series, which includes *Your One-Year-Old, Your Two-Year-Old, Your Three-Year-Old, Your Four-Year-Old, Your Five-Year-Old, Your Six-Year-Old, Your Seven-Year-Old, Your Eight-Year-Old,* and *Your Nine-Year-Old.*)

Bower, S., and G. Bower. *Asserting Your Self.* Reading, MA: Addison-Wesley, 1976.

Foust, Linda. *The Single Parent's Almanac.* Rocklin, CA: Prima, 1996.

Richmond, Gary. *Successful Single Parenting: Going It Alone.* Eugene, OR: Harvest House, 1990.

Time Requirements

This presentation runs from ¾ hour to 1½ hours, depending on the style of the presenter and the number of interactive activities used.

🕐 **Clock symbol.**   This means that the information is included for a longer seminar or workshop. Omit these sections for a shorter presentation. If time is limited, another way to shorten your presentation is to share the information in lecture format. However, keep in mind that it is often harder to engage and maintain the audience's interest with a pure lecture style. Unless you are a particularly dynamic speaker, you will probably want to keep at least a few of the exercises to enliven the presentation.

Video examples.   Showing selected scenes from popular movies is one way to make your presentation more interesting. It creates some variety and interest, stimulates discussion, and may be a way to inject some humor. Consider selecting short scenes from videos such as *Kramer vs. Kramer, Stepmom, Deconstructing Harry,* or *The First Wives' Club.* Suggestions for specific scenes are included in this outline, but you are encouraged to look for other examples on your own as you prepare for your presentation.

Your notes.   Add your own notes and examples to the outline in the spaces provided. Research local support groups and services to add to the two handouts. Consult self-help directories and low-cost counseling services for referral ideas.

How to Use This Presentation

Possible Audiences

Adult education groups at churches and synagogues

PTO/PTA

Women's civic and professional organizations

Whom to Contact

Director of adult education programs

PTO/PTA president

Director of educational programs

Sample Text for Marketing Letter, Brochure, or Postcard

"Single-Parent Survival Skills" is a workshop designed for people raising children without the support and assistance of a partner. It explores ways that single parents can seek and find support for their very challenging situations. Through written exercises and group discussions, participants explore the emotional overload that many single parents experience, ways to enhance the process of recovering from loss, and how to listen to their children with empathy. Participants also discuss a list of 28 strategies designed to help single parents survive and even thrive during their parenting years.

_____ is a licensed _____ in private practice in _____. S/he specializes in _____ and _____. Call _____ today to schedule your group's **free** workshop. (_____) _____-_____.

Sample Text for Press Release

Free Workshop for Single Parents

_____ is presenting "Single-Parent Survival Skills," a workshop designed for people raising children without the support and assistance of a partner. The presentation is scheduled for _____ at _____ in the _____.

The workshop will be led by _____, who says, "Many single parents are on emotional overload. Their lives are very challenging and they always have to be strong. In this workshop, we will discuss a list of 28 strategies designed to help single parents survive and even thrive during their parenting years. It is sure to be an interesting and useful evening for every single parent who attends."

_____ is a licensed _____ in private practice in _____. S/he specializes in _____ and _____. For reservations, call _____ at (_____) _____-_____.

Exhibit 8.1   Presentation Outline

Single-Parent Survival Skills

Topic	*Time Estimate*
I. **Introduction**	2–12 minutes
A. Introduce yourself	
B. Ask group members to introduce themselves	
C. State workshop goals	
II. **Emotional Overload**	2–10 minutes
III. **10 Ways to Speed Your Recovery Process**	7–20 minutes
IV. **Listening Skills**	7–15 minutes
V. **28 Survival Strategies**	20–40 minutes
VI. **Conclusion**	
Approximate Total Time	**38–97 minutes**

Exhibit 8.2   Presentation Script

Single Parent Survival Skills

Outline	Presenter's Comments	Activity
I-A. **Introduce Yourself**	My name is _____. I'm a licensed _____, with a _____. I specialize in working with _____ and _____. About _____ years ago, I became interested in the issues that single parents face. I started noticing that _____ _____.	Refer to your bio on the first page of the handouts. 1 minute.
I-B. **Group Intro** 🕐	I'd like to begin today's workshop by finding out a bit about each of you. Let's go around the room and each of you give your name and tell us what brings you to this workshop.	If the group is under 20 people, ask participants to introduce themselves. 10 minutes.
I-C. **Goals**	This presentation will explore ways that single parents can seek and find support for their very challenging situations. Through written exercises and group discussions, we will talk about the emotional overload that many single parents experience, ways to enhance the process of recovering from loss, and how to listen to your children with empathy. We will also discuss a list of 28 strategies that will help you survive and even thrive during the coming years.	State goals. 1 minute.
II. **Emotional Overload** 🕐	Let's begin with an introduction to this subject by talking about some of the emotions that every single parent experiences at one time or another. What kinds of emotional issues do you have to deal with as a single parent—emotions that you might describe as "extra baggage"?	List all points on a blank easel pad. If time is limited, present information as a lecture. 2–10 minutes.

Answers to look for:

- Self-pity
- Depression
- Guilt
- Anger
- Envy

- Fear
- Severe money problems
- Loneliness and isolation
- Frustration
- Exhaustion

🕐	In the 1979 movie *Kramer vs. Kramer,* Dustin Hoffman plays a father who can't seem to do anything right. In this scene, he attempts to make breakfast for his son.	Show video scene and ask for reactions.

Outline	Presenter's Comments	Activity

In *Successful Single Parenting,* author Gary Richmond calls these issues the extra baggage facing every single parent. These issues present such a challenge because they undermine your daily functioning and emotional well-being. But they can be managed successfully so that you and your children navigate the coming years in a positive way.

III.
10 Ways to
Speed Your
Recovery
Process

Let's look at Handout 8.1, "10 Ways to Speed the Recovery Process."

Let's discuss each of these items. I have some examples of resources offered locally, and I welcome your examples and suggestions.

Handout 8.1.

Discuss all items on handout.

If time is short, present information as a lecture and do not encourage participation.

7–20 minutes.

IV.
Listening
Skills

Item 9 on the previous handout is "Learn to help your kids talk about what is happening to them." Since this is such a critical skill for every single parent, let's look at what it means.

Please complete the exercises on Handout 8.2 by yourself. Give yourself about 5 minutes.

Now that everyone is finished, I'd like to ask people to share their responses. Keep in mind as we go through these that there is no one right answer to any of the questions. The point is to understand the three types of listening skills and get some practice using them.

Handout 8.2.

Participants complete exercise; discuss as a group.

If time is short, provide answers and do not encourage participation.

7–15 minutes.

V.
Survival
Strategies

Let's talk next about Handout 8.3, "28 Single-Parent Survival Strategies." Let's go over each item. As we talk about these, please speak up if you have suggestions or comments.

Note to leader: Have examples of your own prepared before the workshop to make this list more interesting. Examples are provided here as well.

1. Changes often include moving to a new home, changing schools, and so on.

2. Where are places you can go to ask for help?

Handout 8.3.

If time is short, present information as a lecture and do not encourage participation.

20–40 minutes.

Lead discussion.

Ask for examples.

Possible answers:

Relatives, friends, neighbors, teachers, church, and synagogue.

Think of your own examples before the workshop.

What stops you from asking for help?

3. Who has a suggestion on books that outline child development stages? I would like to suggest the series from the Gesell Institute of Human Development or

_____.

4. What feelings are children in single-parent families likely to have?

Answers to look for:

- Uncertainty
- Disappointment
- Grief
- Shame
- Blame
- Abandonment
- Abuse
- Parentification

In the 1998 movie *Stepmom,* actress Jena Malone plays daughter Anna. In this scene, she expresses anger and resentment toward her father (Ed Harris) for leaving her mother and the family.

Show the scene where Anna shouts at her father; ask for reactions.

5. What is the danger of allowing the boundaries to be blurred?

Possible answer:

Children are not allowed to be children. They get the message that they are expected to suppress their own emotions. This is one way they carry their pain into adulthood.

6. What makes it so difficult to accept offers of help?

Possible answers:

- Embarrassment
- Mistrust
- Past hurts
- Greater feeling of safety in relying on yourself

It is not necessary to resolve these issues. Just let participants talk about them

7. What are examples of ways you can lower your expectations?

Possible answers:

- Housekeeping standards
- Amount of money available
- Types of gifts you can buy others

8. What dangers arise when there is inadequate supervision?

Possible answers:

- Boredom
- Sexual behavior
- Alcohol abuse
- Child abuse

9. What are some examples of overly responsible behavior?

Possible answers:

Doing adult chores beyond the norm
Being overly concerned with how the parent is feeling
Never complaining
Not having a social life like other children

To encourage your child to open up, use the skills you learned in the listening skills exercise we did a few minutes ago.

10. How are feelings and behaviors different?

Sample answer:

A child may *feel* sad, lonely, or ashamed. A child may *behave* badly by acting out in destructive ways, such as stealing, lying, or skipping school.

11. Why is flexibility an important survival skill?

Possible answer:

Because many single parents have fewer resources available to them. They usually need to be creative and adaptable to find alternative ways to accomplish their goals.

12. Who has learned to set priorities? What can you tell us about it?

13. Why is it important for single parents to trust their instincts?

Possible answer:

Because most single parents have lower self-esteem and are reluctant to trust their own instincts. Your gut is usually the best place to look when making an important decision.

14. Who would like to share some ways you have simplified your life?

Example to share if no one responds:

It may be better to sell the big house that requires tremendous maintenance and move to a smaller one.

15. Many people don't realize that many therapists and counseling centers offer low-cost services. Don't assume you must pay the full fee. Ask.

16. Ask the group for suggestions on ways to deal with guilt.

Possible answer:

Write about it in your journal. Start with "I feel guilty because . . ." and see what comes out.

17. It can help to make two lists: things you can control and things you can't.

18. Ask the group why rituals are important.

Possible answer:

Rituals enable us to formally acknowledge the ending or passing of something important. This helps us let go.

19. It is very important to have a place to express your private feelings—all of them. It is also critical that you keep the journal in a private place where no one will find it.

20. Ask participants how long they think it should take to recover from a divorce. Point out that there is no *right* amount of time. Your day will come, however, if you work at healing.

21. One way to learn assertiveness is to read one of the classic books on the subject. *Your Perfect Right* and *Asserting Your Self* are classics. (Please see the list of books at the beginning of this outline.)

22. Why is it so important to take care of your body?

Possible answers:

- Your children need you to be there for them.
- You will feel better emotionally if you take care of yourself physically.

Outline	Presenter's Comments	Activity

🕐

In the 1996 movie *The First Wives' Club,* actress Bette Midler plays Brenda, who has been dumped by her husband. In this scene, she speaks with her son (played by Jason Gould) and proudly tells him about the progress she has made. He proceeds to tell her that her former husband is about to get married. She is visibly deflated, but her progress is obvious nonetheless.

Activity: Show the scene where Brenda talks with her son; ask for reactions.

23. If you can't find someone to listen to you, write in your journal.

24. What happens when you don't release that sadness?

Possible answers:

- It builds up and turns to anger.
- It builds up and gets attached to other situations. You become like a walking time bomb.

🕐

In the 1997 movie *Deconstructing Harry,* actress Kirstie Alley provides an example of a walking time bomb. She plays the former wife of Harry Block (Woody Allen). In this scene, she follows him down the street, screaming. (*Warning:* Strong language.)

Activity: Show the scene where Kirstie Alley screams on the street; ask for reactions.

25. Write it on your calendar. Fun is as necessary to your mental health as food is to your body.

26. This can be very therapeutic. Get your fears out of your psyche and into your journal. They will bother you much less.

27. See strategy 26.

28. Single parents often feel like they are not normal. Creating activities where you can remind yourself that you are normal can be therapeutic.

Would anyone like to add any survival strategies to the list?

VI. Conclusion

I hope you have enjoyed today's workshop. In the time remaining, I would be happy to answer any questions you may have.

Activity: Conclude the workshop.

8.11

Handout 8.1   10 Ways to Speed Your Recovery Process

1. Some churches, synagogues, counseling centers, and therapists offer free and low-cost divorce recovery workshops and grief support groups. Look for them in the newspaper and Yellow Pages. If you don't see any listed, call.

    Local examples: _____

    _____

    _____

2. Look for local peer support groups and networks. You may be able to find a local group by calling a national organization such as the following:

    National Organization of Single Mothers
    P.O. Box 68
    Midland, NC 28107
    (704) 888-5063

    Single Parent Resource Center
    141 West 28th Street, Suite 302
    New York, NY 10001
    (212) 947-0221

    Parents Without Partners
    401 N. Michigan Avenue
    Chicago, IL 60611
    (312) 644-6610

    Local examples: _____

    _____

    _____

3. If you have access to the Internet, search for support services in your area.

    Internet addresses: _____

    _____

    _____

4. Also on the Internet, find a chat room or bulletin board where single parents post messages and share ideas.

    Internet addresses: _____

    _____

    _____

5. Find library books for kids about divorce and single parent families, and read them together. Take the time to talk about how they relate to your situation and encourage your kids to talk about their feelings.

   Names of books: _____

   _____

   _____

6. Find a support group for children of divorce.

   Local examples: _____

   _____

   _____

7. Tell your children's teachers and the school psychologist that you are a single-parent family. Let them know that you welcome feedback and suggestions on coping with your circumstances.

8. When you are ready, investigate groups like Parents Without Partners for single adults. You need to be with other adults who have similar interests.

   Local examples: _____

   _____

   _____

9. Learn to help your kids talk about what is happening to them.

10. Learn conflict resolution and problem-solving skills.

Handout 8.2 Listening Skills

Like adults, children have emotional reactions when they lose a parent to divorce or death. The following skills will help you validate and accept your child's feelings, which will help your child deal with his or her struggle.

1. Ask open-ended questions to encourage your partner to talk to you and share his or her feelings.

    Definition: Open-ended questions cannot be answered "yes" or "no." They are phrased to encourage the other person to give a broad response to your question.

    Examples: "How do you feel about what she said?"

    "Tell me all about your day today."

    "What do you think about the new house?"

2. Actively listen to what your child says.

    Definition: Active listening is a two-step response to a statement. It includes reflecting back- what emotion you detected in the statement, and the reason for the emotion.

    Examples: "Sounds like you're pretty excited about visiting Dad next weekend."

    "You're very upset about saying good-bye to Grandma, aren't you?"

3. Summarize what you hear your child telling you. A summary statement enhances your child's self-esteem by showing that you are listening carefully.

    Definition: A statement that summarizes the facts you gathered from your child.

    Examples: "So you're saying you want to go to Cedar Falls before you visit Aunt Emma. Then you want to come home."

    "You're saying that you tried your best, but it was beyond your control."

Practice Exercises

Directions: Choose a listening skill for each situation. Write an example of what you could say to the child to validate his or her feelings and encourage further expression of emotion.

1. Your son comes home from a visit to his father. He is uncharacteristically quiet.

    Which listening skill
    would work best here? _____

    I would say: _____

    _____

2. On the morning of a visit to your ex-wife, your daughter says, "I don't want to go! I hate Mom's boyfriend!"

   Which listening skill
   would work best here? _____

   I would say: _____

   _____

3. Your daughter says, "I can't believe we don't have enough money to go to the Nutcracker. We always used to go!"

   Which listening skill
   would work best here? _____

   I would say: _____

   _____

4. Before he goes to your ex-husband's house for the weekend, your son says, "Please, Mom, please, please let me stay home!"

   Which listening skill
   would work best here? _____

   I would say: _____

   _____

Handout 8.3   28 Single-Parent Survival Strategies

Use the spaces provided to make notes of ideas and things to do.

1. Watch out for too many changes in your life as you recover from both the loss of your spouse and the resulting changes in your life circumstances. Change causes stress, and you have enough right now.

_____

_____

2. Realize and accept that you must get help with your single-parenting responsibilities. It is unrealistic to think that you can do it alone.

_____

_____

3. Manage your own emotions so you will be able to help your child manage his or her struggle. Learn as much as you can about how children respond to the divorce or death of a parent and life in a single-parent home. Do not expect your child to respond the same way you do. Take your child's developmental stage into consideration when responding to his or her behavior.

_____

_____

4. Make it okay for your children to talk to you about their feelings.

_____

_____

5. Keep appropriate boundaries.

   - Don't give in to the temptation to let your child take care of you.
   - Let your children be children.
   - Avoid burdening them with your feelings and the facts of the divorce or death of your spouse.
   - Find another adult to be your sounding board.

_____

_____

6. Let people help you.

   - If it's impossible to reciprocate, say so.
   - People know that your life isn't like it used to be.

- Don't let your inability to reciprocate prevent you from accepting what people willingly offer.

_____

_____

7. Let go of your need for perfection. You will have much more stress if you don't lower your expectations.

_____

_____

8. Even though you are unable to be present as much as in the past, your children still need adult supervision. Look for ways for other adults to look in on your kids when they are home alone, even when they are teenagers.

_____

_____

9. Just because your child appears to be handling his or her emotions well, don't assume that he or she is okay. Some kids respond to the loss of a parent by becoming overly responsible or by closing down their emotions. They may need to hear, "Tell me how you're feeling."

_____

_____

10. While it is important to listen and accept your children's feelings, it is equally important to set limits on behavior.

_____

_____

11. Cultivate your ability to be flexible and find creative ways to solve problems.

_____

_____

12. Learn to set priorities. Do the most important things first.

_____

_____

13. Trust your gut feelings. Pay attention to your instincts and act on them.

_____

_____

14. Simplify as many things as possible in your life. You cannot afford to keep it complicated.

_____

_____

15. Find an outlet for your anger. If a friend is not available, look for a minister, rabbi, or professional counselor. If money is an issue, look for a therapist who will see you for a low fee.

_____

_____

16. Teach yourself to let go of guilt. You don't have time for it, and it's not necessary.

_____

_____

17. Focus on issues you have control over. If something is beyond your control, don't waste your emotions on it.

_____

_____

18. Create a ritual to mark the change in your circumstances. This could be a funeral for your spouse or a ceremony to acknowledge your divorce.

_____

_____

19. Keep a private journal where you express your feelings. Be sure to keep it in a private place where your children won't find it. A journal provides a place to express anger, sadness, loneliness, and fear—all of those feelings you feel every day as a single parent.

_____

_____

20. Remind yourself that recovering from divorce or the death of a spouse will take time. Your recovery will happen on its own schedule, and it will happen. You will get through this intact.

_____

_____

21. Learn to be assertive. You can't say yes to every request, whether it is from your family members or people in the community who want your time and resources. If you give it all away, you will have nothing left for yourself.

_____

_____

22. Find ways to take care of your body. Get regular checkups and make time to exercise. You need rest now more than ever. Watch your alcohol intake.

_____

_____

23. Find someone who will listen to you. Sometimes you have to ask—for example, "I need a sounding board right now. Can I have 15 minutes of your time?"

_____

_____

24. Rent a sad movie and let yourself cry (when the kids aren't around). Crying allows you to release the sadness that you are sure to feel.

_____

_____

25. Do at least one fun thing for yourself every week.

_____

_____

26. In your private journal, make a list of all the things you're afraid of.

_____

_____

27. In your private journal, make a list of all the things you worry about.

_____

_____

28. Get together with other single-parent families. Sharing time with people facing similar issues can make you feel normal.

_____

_____

Note other strategies here:

_____

_____

_____

_____

Chapter 9

Minimizing the Emotional Toll of Divorce

Presentation Synopsis

This presentation is designed for people who are experiencing the stresses of divorce. It focuses on the following topics: how divorce affects both adults and children; how to recognize and minimize emotional distress in children; survival strategies for the divorcing adult; and how to recognize when one should consider seeking emotional support.

This presentation is based, in part, on information from the following books. I recommend that you review them as you prepare your presentation:

Bridges, William. *Transitions: Making Sense of Life's Changes.* New York, Addison-Wesley, 1980.

Engel, Marjorie, and Diana Gould. *The Divorce Decisions Workbook.* New York, McGraw-Hill, 1992, p. 109.

Trafford, Abigail. *Crazy Time: Surviving Divorce and Building a New Life.* New York, HarperCollins, 1992.

Wallerstein, Judith, and Joan Berlin Kelly. *Surviving the Breakup: How Children and Parents Cope with Divorce.* New York, Basic Books, 1980.

Time Requirements

This presentation runs from 1 to 2 hours, depending on the style of the presenter and the number of interactive activities used.

⏱ **Clock symbol.**   This means that the information is included for a longer seminar or workshop. Omit these sections for a shorter presentation. If time is limited, another way to shorten your presentation is to share the information in lecture format. However, keep in mind that it is often harder to engage and maintain the audience's interest with a pure lecture style. Unless you are a particularly dynamic speaker, you will probably want to keep at least a few of the exercises to enliven the presentation.

How to Use This Presentation

Possible Audiences	**Whom to Contact**
Adult education groups at churches and synagogues	Director of adult education programs
PTO/PTA	PTO/PTA president
Women's civic and professional organizations	Director of educational programs

Sample Text for Marketing Letter, Brochure, or Postcard

As a licensed mental health professional, I work with many individuals, couples, and families who are affected by divorce. I see the devastating effects that divorce can have on people and am dedicated to helping people develop coping skills. I am offering to present a workshop titled "Minimizing the Emotional Toll of Divorce" for your members as a community service.

In this workshop, participants learn how divorce affects both adults and children. They learn how to recognize and minimize emotional distress in children and explore survival strategies for the divorcing adult. They also learn how to recognize when they should consider seeking emotional support.

_____ is a licensed _____ in private practice in _____. S/he specializes in _____ and _____. Call _____ today to schedule your group's free workshop. (_____) _____-_____.

Sample Text for Press Release

_____ Presents "Minimizing the Emotional Toll of Divorce"

_____ is presenting a **free** workshop on how to minimize the emotional toll of divorce. The workshop is scheduled for _____, from _____ to _____ at _____. The workshop is limited to ____ participants and is open to the public. This presentation will focus on how divorce affects both adults and children. Participants will learn how to recognize and minimize emotional distress in children, and learn survival strategies for the divorcing adult. They will also learn how to recognize when a person should consider seeking emotional support.

_____ is a licensed _____ in private practice in _____. S/he specializes in _____ and _____. For reservations, call _____ at (_____) _____-_____.

Exhibit 9.1   Presentation Outline

Minimizing the Emotional Toll of Divorce

Topic	*Time Estimate*
I. Introduction	2–12 minutes
A. Introduce yourself	
B. Ask group members to introduce themselves	
C. State workshop goals	
II. How Divorce Causes Disruption	6–10 minutes
III. How Divorce Affects Adults	5–10 minutes
IV. How Divorce Affects Children	5–10 minutes
V. Signs of Emotional Distress in Children	5–10 minutes
VI. How to Minimize the Emotional Impact of Divorce on Children	10–20 minutes
VII. Survival Strategies for the Divorcing Adult	20–40 minutes
VIII. How to Recognize When You Should Seek Help	5–10 minutes
IX. Conclusion	
Approximate Total Time	**58–122 minutes**

Exhibit 9.2   Presentation Script

Minimizing the Emotional Toll of Divorce

Outline	Presenter's Comments	Activity
I-A. **Introduce** **Yourself**	My name is _____. I'm a licensed _____, with a _____. I specialize in working with _____, and became interested in helping people who were experiencing the stresses of divorce. This is especially important to me because _____.	Refer to your bio on the first page of the handouts. 1 minute.
I-B. **Group Intro** 🕐	I'd like to begin today's workshop by finding out a bit about each of you. Let's go around the room and each of you tell us your name and something about yourself.	If the group is under 20 people, ask participants to introduce themselves. 10 minutes.
I-C. **Goals**	In this workshop, we will look at how divorce affects both adults and children; how to recognize and minimize emotional distress in children; survival strategies for the divorcing adult; and how to recognize when you should consider seeking the help of a mental health professional.	State goals. 1 minute.
II. **How Divorce** **Causes** **Disruption** 🕐	The decision to divorce causes major changes in the lives of all family members. Some upheaval is inevitable. The four main kinds of disruption are: 1. *Financial.* Money becomes a huge problem for most people. The cost of a divorce is extremely high, and two households cost more than one. 2. *Career.* Being less focused at work and spending time away from the job for divorce-related appointments takes its toll. 3. *Logistics.* Running your home is more difficult because you no longer have a partner to help with daily chores. 4. *Emotional.* Most people have periods of depression, sadness, anger, and fatigue. Are there any issues you would add to this list?	Present information. 6–10 minutes. If time allows, ask for comments and examples. If time is limited, present information as a lecture and don't encourage discussion.

Outline	Presenter's Comments	Activity

III.
How Divorce
Affects
Adults
🕐

In *Crazy Time,* author Abigail Trafford describes the emotional effects of divorce as follows:

"This is Crazy Time. It starts when you separate and usually lasts about two years. It's a time when your emotions take on a life of their own and you swing back and forth between wild euphoria and violent anger, ambivalence and deep depression, extreme timidity and rash actions. You are not yourself. Who are you? At times you don't want to know."

These are the kinds of feelings adults report as they experience the divorce process:

- Poor concentration
- Nightmares
- Sleep problems
- Fatigue
- Mood swings

- Feeling tense
- Nausea
- Gaining or losing weight
- Feeling nervous
- Somatic complaints

Are there any feelings you would add to this list?

Activity: Present information.

5–10 minutes.

If time allows, ask for examples and discussion.

If time is limited, present information as a lecture and don't encourage discussion.

IV.
How Divorce
Affects
Children
🕐

Divorce profoundly affects children. In *Surviving the Breakup,* author Judith Wallerstein describes the experience of 60 divorcing families. She outlines the following "central themes of the child's divorce experience":

Fear.   Divorce is frightening to children, and they respond with anxiety. Children feel more vulnerable after a divorce because their world has become less reliable.

Fear of abandonment.   One-third of the children in Wallerstein's study feared that their mother would abandon them.

Confusion.   The children in divorcing families become confused about their relationships with their parents. They see their parents' relationship fall apart and sometimes conclude that their own relationship with one or both parents could dissolve, as well.

Sadness and yearning.   More than half of the children in the Wallerstein study were openly tearful and sad in response to the losses they experienced. Two-thirds expressed yearning, for example: "We need a daddy. We don't have a daddy."

Activity: Present information.

5–10 minutes.

If time allows, ask for examples and discussion.

If time is limited, present information as a lecture and don't encourage discussion.

Worry.   In Wallerstein's study, many children expressed concern about one or both of their parents' ability to cope with their lives. They wondered if their parents were emotionally stable and able to make it on their own.

Over half of the children expressed deep worries about their mothers. They witnessed their mothers' mood swings and emotional reactions to the events in the family. Some children worried about suicide and accidents.

Feeling rejected.   Many children who experience a parent moving out of the home feel rejected by the parent. The parent is usually preoccupied with problems and pays less attention to the child than in the past. Many children take this personally and feel rejected and unlovable.

Loneliness.   Since both parents are preoccupied with their own problems during the divorce process, they are less able to fulfill their parenting roles with their children. The children may feel that their parents are slipping away from them. If the father has moved away and mother has gone off to work, the children often feel profound loneliness.

Divided loyalties.   The children may (accurately) perceive that the parents are in a battle with each other. The children feel pulled in both directions and may resolve the dilemma by siding with one parent against another.

Anger.   Children in divorcing families experience more aggression and anger. It is often directed toward the parents, expressed in tantrums, irritability, resentment, and verbal attacks. Many children see the divorce as a selfish act and feel very resentful about the resulting destruction of their lives.

V.
Signs of
Emotional
Distress in
Children

More than one-third of the children in Judith Wallerstein's study showed acute depressive symptoms such as sleeplessness, restlessness, difficulty in concentrating, deep sighing, feelings of emptiness, compulsive overeating, and various somatic complaints.

The symptoms that many children may have during the divorce process either moderate or disappear within 18 months after the breakup. Of the symptoms that remain, the most common are:

Present information.

5–10 minutes.

If time allows, ask for comments and examples.

If time is limited, present information as a lecture and don't encourage discussion.

Outline	Presenter's Comments	Activity

1. *Manipulative behavior* was reported by about 20 percent of the teachers of the children in Wallerstein's study.

2. *Intense anger* at one or both parents was reported by 25 percent of the children and adolescents 1 year after the divorce.

3. Depression was diagnosed in 25 percent of the children and adolescents. The symptoms of depression in children include:

- Low self-esteem
- Inability to concentrate
- Sadness
- Mood swings
- Irritability
- Secretiveness
- Isolation
- Self-blame
- Eating disorders
- Perfect behavior
- Tendency to be accident-prone
- Stealing
- Truancy from school
- Underachievement at school
- Sexual acting out

VI.
How to Minimize the Emotional Impact of Divorce on Children 🕐

Please take a look at Handout 9.1, "Children's Divorce Rights."

Let's go through this list and discuss each item. I'd like your reactions and comments about each one.

Handout 9.1.

10–20 minutes.

Read each item and ask for examples and comments. Or, if time is limited, read items and don't elicit comments.

VII.
Survival Strategies for the Divorcing Adult 🕐

Please take a look at Handout 9.2, "36 Divorce Survival Strategies."

Let's go through this list and discuss each item. I'd like your reactions and comments about each one.

Handout 9.2.

20–40 minutes.

Read each item and ask for examples and comments. Or, if time is limited, read items and don't elicit comments.

Outline	Presenter's Comments	Activity
VIII. **How to** **Recognize** **When to Seek** **Help** 🕐	You should consider finding a therapist to work with if you are experiencing the following feelings and symptoms most of the time: ● Loneliness ● Feeling overwhelmed by your children ● Depression ● Feeling overwhelmed by your feelings ● Numbness ● Sleeping too much or too little ● Exhaustion ● Worry ● Isolation ● Anxiousness ● Hopelessness ● Fear	Present information. 5–10 minutes. Read each item and ask for examples and comments. Or, if time is limited, read items and don't elicit comments.
IX. **Conclusion**	I hope you have learned something from my presentation today. In the time remaining, I would be happy to answer any questions you may have.	Conclude the workshop.

Handout 9.1 Children's Divorce Rights

The following list of rights is adapted from the Bill of Rights of Children in Divorce Actions. It was created by the Honorable Robert Hansen, based on decisions of the Wisconsin Supreme Court.

Children have the following rights during the divorce process:

1. Children have the right to be treated as an interested and affected person—not as a pawn, possession, or chattel of either or both parents.

2. Children have the right to the day-by-day love, care, discipline, and protection of the parent having custody of the child.

3. Children have the right to know the noncustodial parent, and to benefit from the parent's love and guidance through an appropriate amount of contact.

4. Children have the right to a positive and constructive relationship with both parents. Neither parent should be allowed to degrade or downgrade the other in the mind of the child.

5. Children have the right to learn moral and ethical values. Limits should be set on children's behavior early in life, to assist them in developing self-discipline and self-control.

6. Children have the right to an adequate level of economic support provided by both parents.

7. Children have the right to the same educational opportunities as they would have had without a divorce.

8. Children have the right to have their custody and child support arrangements reviewed periodically.

9. Children have the right to be acknowledged as disadvantaged people who need the protection of the law.

10. Children have the right to be free to contact their absent parents when they wish to do so.

11. Children have the right to form close relationships with each parent's new friends.

Source: Marjorie Engel and Diana Gould, *The Divorce Decisions Workbook* (New York, McGraw-Hill, 1992), p. 109. Reproduced with permission.

1. Take your time. Recognize that you are going through a major life transition that cannot be rushed.

2. Set up temporary arrangements to help yourself get through the changes involved in your divorce process.

3. You will frequently feel frustrated. Avoid the temptation of acting for the sake of acting just because it gives you a temporary feeling of being in control.

4. Slow down and identify why you feel uncomfortable.

5. Don't force any more changes on yourself than are necessary.

6. Explore both the benefits and costs of your new life.

7. In your journal, think about the future. Explore the question, "What is waiting to happen in my life now?"

8. Remember to ask yourself, "What am I supposed to learn from this?"

9. Protect yourself against the inevitable forgetfulness and absent-mindedness that many divorcing people report. Make a list of important account numbers, telephone numbers, and so on and keep them in a safe place.

10. Watch out for too many changes in your life as you recover from the divorce and the changes in your life circumstances. Change causes stress, and you have enough right now.

11. Let people help you.
    - If it's impossible to reciprocate, say so.
    - People know that your life isn't like it used to be.
    - Don't let your inability to reciprocate prevent you from accepting what people willingly offer.

12. Let go of your need for perfection. You will not survive unless you lower your expectations.

13. Cultivate your ability to be flexible and find creative ways to solve problems.

14. Learn to set priorities. Do the most important things first.

15. Trust your gut feelings. Pay attention to your instincts and act on them.

16. Simplify everything in your life. You cannot afford to keep it complicated.

17. Find an outlet for your anger. If a friend is not available, look for a minister, rabbi, or professional counselor. If money is an issue, look for a therapist who will see you for a low fee.

18. Teach yourself to let go of guilt. You don't have time for it, and it's not necessary.

19. Focus on issues you have control over. If something is beyond your control, don't waste your emotions on it.

20. Create a ceremony to acknowledge your divorce.

21. Learn to be assertive. You can't say yes to every request, whether it is from your family members or people in the community who want your time and resources. If you give it all away, you will have nothing left for yourself.

22. Find ways to take care of your body. Get regular checkups and make time to exercise. You need rest now more than ever. Watch your alcohol intake.

23. Find someone who will listen to you. Sometimes you have to ask—for example, "I need a sounding board right now. Can I have 15 minutes of your time?"

24. Rent a sad movie and let yourself cry (when the kids aren't around). Crying allows you to release the sadness that you are sure to feel.

25. Do at least one fun thing for yourself every week.

26. In your private journal, make a list of all the things you're afraid of.

27. In your private journal, make a list of all the things you worry about.

If you have children:

28. Manage your own emotions so you will be able to help your child manage his or her struggle.

   - Learn as much as you can about how children respond to divorce and life in a single parent home.
   - Do not expect your child to respond the same way you do.
   - Take your child's developmental stage into consideration when responding to his or her behavior.

29. Make it okay for your children to talk to you about their feelings.

30. Keep appropriate boundaries.

   - Don't give in to the temptation to let your child take care of you.
   - Let your children be children.
   - Avoid burdening them with your feelings and the facts of the divorce.
   - Find another adult to be your sounding board.

31. Even though you may be unable to be present as much as in the past, your children still need adult supervision. Look for ways for other adults to look in on your kids when they are home alone, even when they are teenagers.

32. Just because your child appears to be handling his or her emotions well, don't assume that he or she is okay. Some kids respond to divorce by becoming overly responsible or by closing down their emotions. They may need to hear, "Tell me how you're feeling."

33. While it is important to listen and accept your children's feelings, it is equally important to set limits on behavior.

34. Keep a private journal where you express your feelings. Be sure to keep it in a private place where your children won't find it. A journal provides a place to express anger, sadness, loneliness, and fear—all of those feelings you feel every day as a single parent.

35. Remind yourself that recovering from divorce will take time. Your recovery will happen on its own schedule, and it will happen. You will get through this intact.

36. Get together with other single-parent families. Sharing times with people facing similar issues can make you feel normal.

Note other strategies here:

_____

_____

_____

_____

_____

_____

_____

_____

_____

_____

_____

_____

_____

_____

_____

_____

Chapter 10

Avoiding Emotional Disasters: Just for Teens

Presentation Synopsis

This workshop is designed for teenagers. Through written exercises and group discussion, participants will learn strategies for surviving and thriving during the teen years. They will discuss how to manage the emotional roller coaster of mood swings and loneliness, as well as how to prevent and manage stress overload.

This presentation is based partly on information found in the following books. I recommend that you review them as you prepare your presentation:

Kelly, Kate. *The Complete Idiot's Guide to Parenting a Teenager.* New York: Alpha Books, 1996.

Law, Felicia, and Josephine Parker, eds. *Growing Up: A Young Person's Guide to Adolescence.* Chippenham, Wiltshire, U.K.: Merlion, 1993.

McCoy, Kathy, and Charles Wibbelsman. *The New Teenage Body Book.* New York: Putnam, 1992.

Time Requirements

This presentation runs from 1 hour to 1½ hours, depending on the style of the presenter and the number of interactive activities used.

🕐 **Clock symbol.**   This means that the information is included for a longer seminar or workshop. Omit these sections for a shorter presentation. If time is limited, another way to shorten your presentation is to share the information in lecture format. However, keep in mind that it is often harder to engage and maintain the audience's interest with a pure lecture style. Unless you are a particularly dynamic speaker, you will probably want to keep at least a few of the exercises to enliven the presentation.

How to Use This Presentation

Possible Audiences

Teen groups at churches and synagogues

High school and middle school (home economics, psychology, sociology, etc.)

Whom to Contact

Director of youth programs

Teachers of specific classes, school social worker, school psychologist, or guidance counselor

Sample Text for Marketing Letter, Brochure, or Postcard

Would your students/members value a personal growth workshop designed especially for teens? _____ is offering an educational and motivational seminar to your group as a community service. Through written exercises and group discussion, participants in this workshop will learn strategies for surviving and thriving during the teen years. They will discuss how to manage the emotional roller coaster of mood swings and loneliness, as well as how to prevent and manage stress overload.

_____ is a licensed _____ in private practice in _____. S/he specializes in _____ and _____. Call _____ today to schedule your group's free workshop. (_____) _____-_____.

Sample Text for Press Release

_____ Presents "Avoiding Emotional Disasters: Just for Teens"

_____ is presenting a **free** workshop to help teens survive and thrive during the high school years. The workshop is scheduled for _____, from _____ to _____ at _____. The workshop is limited to ____ participants and is open to the public.

According to _____, "The teen years are an enormous emotional challenge for most people. But there are things teens can do to make it a positive experience. In this workshop, we will explore ways to manage the emotional roller coaster and deal with stress."

_____ is a licensed _____ in private practice in _____. S/he specializes in _____ and _____. For reservations, call _____ at (_____) _____-_____.

Exhibit 10.1   Presentation Outline

Avoiding Emotional Disasters: Just for Teens

Topic	*Time Estimate*
I. **Introduction**	2–12 minutes
A. Introduce yourself	
B. Ask group members to introduce themselves	
C. State workshop goals	
II. **12 Strategies for Surviving and Thriving during the Teen Years**	54–74 minutes
III. **Managing the Emotional Roller Coaster**	3–8 minutes
IV. **Managing Mood Swings**	3–8 minutes
V. **Managing Loneliness**	3–8 minutes
VI. **Managing Stress Overload**	3–8 minutes
VII. **Conclusion**	
Approximate Total Time	**68–118 minutes**

Exhibit 10.2 Presentation Script

Avoiding Emotional Disasters: Just for Teens

Outline	Presenter's Comments	Activity
I-A. **Introduce** **Yourself**	My name is _____. I'm a licensed _____, with a _____. I specialize in working with _____, and _____. I first became interested in helping adolescents navigate the teenage years when _____. I saw that some teens seem to have much less trouble than others, and wondered why that was. I began studying this _____ ago, when _____ _____ _____.	Refer to your bio on the first page of the handouts. 1 minute.
I-B. **Group Intro**	I'd like to begin today's workshop by finding out a bit about each of you. Let's go around the room and each of you tell us your name and share two things: the name of your favorite musical group and the worst thing about being a teen.	If the group is under 20 people, ask participants to introduce themselves. List names of musical groups and worst things about being a teen on a blank easel page. 10 minutes.
I-C. **Goals**	In this workshop, we will explore what's the hardest about being a teen and ways to make it easier on yourself. We will talk about why life is such an emotional challenge at times, and what you can do to make it less stressful. With the strategies we'll be talking about, you may even *enjoy* your teen years.	State goals. 1 minute.
II. 12 **Survival** **Strategies**	Handout 10.1 lists the 12 strategies we'll be discussing. Let's begin with the first one. 1. *Understand what emotional changes to expect.* It always helps to know what you're getting into. When you know what to expect, the changes of adolescence don't come as such a surprise. It's like seeing the trailer before you see the movie, or reading the table of contents before you start a book. It gives you a sense of what's to come, so you feel prepared.	Handout 10.1. Present information. 2 minutes.

2. *Get to know yourself better.*   The teen years can be very confusing. You often may feel like you're not the same person you were when you got up this morning. How do you keep track of your changing self? One way is to keep a journal—a private notebook where you write about your feelings.

Handout 10.2 provides some ideas for things to explore in your journal. You will feel less confused if you take the time to explore how you feel about some of these things.

Choose one of the statements on Handout 10.2 and write about it. Take about two minutes. When you are finished, I'll ask two or three people to share what they wrote.

Let's return now to Handout 10.1 and continue with the list.

Handout 10.2.

Write responses.

2 minutes.

Group discussion.

5 minutes.

3. *Look for positive influences.*   How would you define *role model?*

Answers to look for:

- Mentor
- Good example
- Someone to pattern yourself after

Group discussion.

Ask for examples and encourage discussion.

15 minutes.

Write suggestions on blank easel page.

Role models are important because they set an example for you to follow. If you admire someone and model yourself after him or her, it can give you some direction and some goals.

Who are some positive influences in your life?

Answers to look for:

Examples of family members, teachers, leaders, and famous people.

4. *Practice thinking for yourself.*   How can you tell when someone is thinking for him- or herself?

Answer to look for:

He or she asks questions.

Thinking for yourself is a sign of strong self-esteem. It means that you know you matter, and that you value your ability to think.

What is the difference between asking questions and politely taking direction? Are there times when it is better to just do what you are told, or is it always better to question?

Discussion points to look for:

- Timing is important.
- In some situations (such as the workplace), it may be more appropriate to take direction without asking questions.
- *How* a question is asked may be as important as *what* is asked.

5. *Learn to be assertive.* Assertive behavior is another sign of self-esteem. It usually means that a person values him or herself. Handout 10.3 provides definitions for assertive behavior and contrasts it with passive and aggressive behavior.

Handout 10.3.

Complete the practice exercises.

10 minutes.

Take about 10 minutes to complete the practice exercises on this handout. When you are finished, we will talk about each one together.

Let's discuss them now . . .

(If time is limited, participants may complete this exercise on their own later.)

Discuss responses.

Now let's go back to Handout 10.1.

6. *Learn to present yourself with confidence.*

Written exercise.

4 minutes.

Make a list of at least five things you do well. Write them down on the back of one of your handouts. Take about 2 minutes.

Next, make a list of at least five things you don't do very well. Write them down on the back of one of your handouts. Take about 2 more minutes.

What kinds of things did you include on your list?

In *Growing Up: A Young Person's Guide To Adolescence,* the authors suggest that you develop your confidence by making two lists like you just did. They suggest that you do something from the first list every day, which will make you feel good about yourself. Then, when you're feeling good, do something from the second list. You will see that the way you feel about yourself at the moment can greatly affect how you perform.

Ask 2–3 people to share briefly.

1 minute.

Present information.

7. *Learn to express your opinions.*　Let's take a look at each point on Handout 10.4.

- *Think about what you want to say before you say it.* Organize your facts and arguments.

- *Wait until the other person is receptive to hearing your ideas.*　Having good timing can make a huge difference in the impact your statement makes.

- *Present yourself in a friendly, nonthreatening way.* People will be more receptive to you if you smile.

- *Listen to what the other person says.*　If someone responds to you, listen to his or her message.

- *Pay attention to how your voice sounds.*　Speak clearly and not too loudly.

- *State your opinion in a friendly and courteous way.* Being rude or unfriendly turns people off and lessens your impact.

- *Stick to the facts.*　Facts will help you win your argument.

- *Recognize that there are a variety of ways of seeing any situation.*　People may not agree with you. You have more power when you acknowledge that others have a right to a different point of view.

- *Acknowledge the other point of view.*　People may not agree with you. You have more power when you acknowledge that others have a right to a different point of view.

Let's go back to Handout 10.1.

8. *Find out what you believe in.*　One of the tasks of adolescence is to find out what you believe in—what you value in life. This process involves questioning the ideas of people around you, especially your parents. It is understandable that you will reject some of your parents' values and beliefs, but there are constructive ways of disagreeing.

What are some nonproductive ways of disagreeing with parents and other authority figures?

Activity column:

Handout 10.4.

Present information.

5 minutes.

Present information and encourage discussion.

10–20 minutes.

If time is limited, ask fewer questions.

Outline	*Presenter's Comments*	*Activity*

Answers to look for:

- Temper tantrums
- Violence
- Rebelling
- Disobeying laws

List ideas on a blank easel page.

What are more productive ways to disagree?

Answers to look for:

- Negotiation
- Forming or joining an action group

List ideas on a blank easel page.

9. *Create your own private place.* As you grow older, you have a greater need for a private place that is all you own. You need it as a place to escape to, but also as a place where you can create your own life.

At the end of adolescence, you will be an adult, ready to go out into the world. You will need to be ready to stand on your own, as an independent and responsible person. What are some of the things you need to be able to call your own?

Answers to look for:

- Private space
- Place to play music
- Place to study and read
- Your journal
- Places to meet friends
- Money
- Possessions

List ideas on a blank easel page.

10. *Make a few good friends.* Making new friends takes some effort. Some people seem to make friends quite easily, while others find it difficult. It's mostly a matter of learning a few skills.

What are some of your ideas for meeting and making new friends?

Answers to look for:

- Smile; appear friendly.
- Say "Hi."
- Ask questions.
- Give compliments.
- Join groups.
- Ask for information ("Where did you get your jacket?").
- Be interested.

List ideas on a blank easel page.

10.9

Let's continue with the points on Handout 10.1.

11. *Find someone you can talk to.*   Just in case you
    hadn't noticed, adolescence is a highly emotional
    time. You are learning new things every day and you
    are not always ready to meet the demands of social
    situations. It's very important to have someone you
    can talk to during this time. Different people can help
    you with different kinds of problems. The important
    thing is that when you start to feel stressed, it means
    you probably need to let it out.

    What are some examples of people who can help you
    when you need to talk?

List ideas on a
blank easel page.

Answers to look for:

- Parents
- Siblings
- Relatives
- Minister or rabbi
- Doctors
- Psychotherapists
- Police officers
- Teachers
- School psychologist
- Guidance counselor
- Your friends
- Friends' parents
- Neighbors

12. *Learn teamwork skills.*   What are examples of
    teamwork skills?

List ideas on a
blank easel page.

Answers to look for:

- Cooperating
- Trust
- Decision making
- Planning
- Supporting
- Encouraging
- Problem solving
- Demonstrating loyalty

Why are teamwork skills important? What benefits do
you gain from developing them?

List ideas on a
blank easel page.

Answers to look for:

- Learn to get along in any kind of group.
- Meet new kinds of people.
- Build courage.
- Build confidence.
- Gain sense of security.
- Gain sense of belonging.

Outline	Presenter's Comments	Activity
III. **Managing the** **Emotional** **Roller** **Coaster** ⏱	One of the tasks of adolescence is learning to manage your emotions. You will feel things you never felt as a child, and it can be very confusing. Take a look next at Handout 10.5 as we talk about this. You can write some of these things down if you want to.	Handout 10.5. Present information. 10–30 minutes.
IV. **Managing** **Mood Swings** ⏱	Mood swings are normal. Feeling happy one minute and sad the next is common during adolescence. Learning to cope with mood swings can be a challenge, though. I'm going to give you a few suggestions, and you may want to list them on Handout 10.5. If you think of a few more as we discuss these, please share them with everyone.	Ask questions and encourage discussion if enough time is available.

1. Accept your feelings as normal. Everyone feels angry or sad from time to time.
2. Talk about your feelings. Use the support network, such as the people we mentioned earlier in this workshop.
3. Write about your feelings in your journal.
4. Get some physical exercise. It can relieve a lot of the pressure.
5. Cry.
6. Go for a long walk or a run.
7. Find a place where you won't disturb (or scare) anyone. Shout, scream or cry. Let it out without hurting anyone else.
8. If you are feeling bad most of the time, or it lasts more than a few weeks, you may need help. Ask your parents or get help from your school counselor or psychologist.

	What other suggestions do you have for dealing with mood swings?	If time allows, ask for more ideas and encourage discussion.
V. **Managing** **Loneliness** ⏱	Loneliness is what you feel when you are alone and don't want to be. It's normal to feel lonely at certain times, like when your best friend is away on vacation. But if you feel lonely at other times, these suggestions may help. You may want to list them on Handout 10.5. If you think of a few more as we discuss these, please share them.	

1. Feeling lonely may be a sign that your self-esteem is low. Ask yourself why you are feeling bad about yourself. Write about it in your journal or talk to a trusted person about your feelings.

2. Make a list of 20 things that you like about yourself. Sometimes it helps to remind yourself that you are a good person and other people like you.

Outline	Presenter's Comments	Activity

3. Turn your attention to someone else. Ask questions and listen carefully.

4. Get involved in a structured activity where you will be around others. Find a place where you are needed. Join a group, get a job, or volunteer.

What other suggestions do you have for dealing with loneliness?

If time allows, ask for more ideas and encourage discussion.

VI.
Managing
Stress
Overload

Life can be very stressful for adolescents. It can make you feel irritable, make it hard to concentrate, cause sleep problems, and even cause headaches or stomach problems. When you are feeling the symptoms of stress overload, it is important to take action.

I have a few suggestions for dealing with this, and you may want to list them on Handout 10.5. If you think of a few more as we discuss these, please share them with us.

1. See a doctor for physical problems like headaches and stomach aches.
2. Get regular exercise.
3. Avoid junk food. It makes the stress reaction worse.
4. Talk about it. Use your support systems.
5. Take a break. Don't try to do so much.
6. Write in your journal. Are you expecting yourself to be superman or superwoman?
7. Do something fun.

What other suggestions do you have for managing stress?

If time allows, ask for more ideas and encourage discussion.

VII.
Conclusion

I hope you have enjoyed today's workshop. In the time remaining, I would be happy to answer any questions you may have.

Conclude the workshop.

Handout 10.1   12 Survival Strategies for Teens

1. Understand what emotional changes to expect.

_____

_____

_____

2. Get to know yourself better.

_____

_____

_____

3. Look for positive influences.

_____

_____

_____

4. Practice thinking for yourself.

_____

_____

_____

5. Learn to be assertive.

_____

_____

_____

6. Learn to present yourself with confidence.

_____

_____

_____

7. Learn to express your opinions.

_____

_____

_____

8. Find out what you believe in.

_____

_____

_____

9. Create your own private place.

_____

_____

_____

10. Make a few good friends.

_____

_____

_____

11. Find someone you can talk to.

_____

_____

_____

12. Learn teamwork skills.

_____

_____

_____

Handout 10.2   Who Am I?

The following questions can help you explore your feelings. This is especially helpful when you're feeling confused.

I like the following things about myself:

_____

_____

_____

I felt happy when . . .

_____

_____

_____

I felt sad when . . .

_____

_____

_____

I was angry when . . .

_____

_____

_____

Someday I hope I can . . .

_____

_____

_____

I wish I had . . .

_____

_____

_____

I wish I had never . . .

_____

_____

_____

I wish I had the courage to . . .

_____

_____

_____

In 10 years, I . . .

_____

_____

_____

In 20 years, I . . .

_____

_____

_____

I know I'll never . . .

_____

_____

_____

I plan to develop my ability to . . .

_____

_____

_____

Handout 10.3   Assertive Behavior

Assertive behavior enables you to:

- Act in your own best interests
- Stand up for yourself without becoming anxious
- Express your honest feelings
- Assert your personal rights, without denying the rights of others

Assertive behavior is:

- Self-expressive
- Honest
- Direct
- Self-enhancing
- Not harmful to others
- Appropriate to the person and situation rather than universal
- Socially responsible
- A combination of learned skills, not an inborn trait

Assertive behavior includes both *what* you say and *how* you say it.

Assertive, Aggressive, or Passive?

Read each of the following conversations and decide whether each illustrates aggressive, passive, or assertive behavior.

Example #1

SUSAN: Listen, I've got a big problem with what you did. I've had it with these stupid mistakes. You either stop screwing up, or you're finished!

GEORGE: Give me a break, Susan. You know it wasn't my fault.

SUSAN: Yeah, right! All I ever hear from you is excuses!

GEORGE: Those aren't excuses, Susan. They're facts.

SUSAN: When are you going to do it the way I told you to do it?

Susan's behavior is: _____

Example #2

SUSAN: George, I wish you'd be more careful with these numbers.

GEORGE: I told you, Susan, it wasn't my fault.

SUSAN: Oh, I'm sorry. You're right.

Susan's behavior is: _____

Example #3

SUSAN: George, these mistakes created a big problem for me. I ended up sending in the wrong information and now I feel very embarrassed.

GEORGE: I told you, Susan, it wasn't my fault.

SUSAN: I know you've had some problems, George. But I have to ask you to double-check your reports in the future, and sign at the bottom to show that you vouch for its accuracy. Will you agree to do that?

GEORGE: Sure, I think I can agree to that.

SUSAN: Thanks, George. I hope this solves the problem.

Susan's behavior is: _____

Source: Robert Alberti and Michael Emmons, *Your Perfect Right,* 7th ed. (Atascadero, CA: Impact, 1995).

Handout 10.4   Your Opinion Counts

If you follow these guidelines when you express your opinion, you will enhance the probability that you will be heard and understood.

1. Think about what you want to say before you say it.

    _____

    _____

2. Wait until the other person is receptive to hearing your ideas.

    _____

    _____

3. Present yourself in a friendly, nonthreatening way.

    _____

    _____

4. Listen to what the other person says.

    _____

    _____

5. Pay attention to how your voice sounds.

    _____

    _____

6. State your opinion in a friendly and courteous way.

    _____

    _____

7. Stick to the facts.

    _____

    _____

8. Recognize that there are a variety of ways of seeing any situation.

    _____

    _____

Handout 10.5　Managing Your Emotions

Mood swings are: _____

I can handle my moods by:

_____

_____

_____

_____

When I feel lonely, I can:

_____

_____

_____

_____

I can relieve stress by:

_____

_____

_____

_____

Chapter 11

Managing Conflict Creatively

Presentation Synopsis

Every relationship has conflicts. In some relationships, conflict is a serious problem, while in others, differences are resolved without creating a major incident. This workshop explores how people resolve their conflicts, the effects conflicts have on relationships and families, and how we learn to manage differences as we do. Participants also learn skills for resolving and preventing conflicts.

This presentation is based partly on information found in the following book. I recommend that you review it as you prepare your presentation:

Bower, Sharon, and Gordon Bower. *Asserting Yourself.* New York: Addison-Wesley, 1976.

Time Requirements

This presentation runs from 1 hour to 1½ hours, depending on the style of the presenter and the number of interactive activities used.

🕐 **Clock symbol.** This means that the information is included for a longer presentation. Omit these sections when time is limited. Another way to shorten your presentation is to make use of the lecture format. However, keep in mind that it is often harder to engage and maintain the audience's interest with a pure lecture style. Unless you are an especially dynamic speaker, you will probably want to keep at least a few of the exercises to enliven the presentation.

Video examples. Showing selected scenes from popular movies is one way to make your presentation more interesting. It creates some variety and interest, stimulates discussion, and may be a way to inject some humor. Consider selecting short scenes from videos such as *Alice in Wonderland, Ordinary People,* and *Waiting to Exhale.* Suggestions for specific scenes are included in this outline, but you are encouraged to look for other examples on your own as you prepare for your presentation. Be sure to have the videos cued up before your participants arrive. Make certain you know how to operate all audiovisual equipment before you begin your presentation.

How to Use This Presentation

Possible Audiences	**Whom to Contact**
PTO or PTA	President or program chairperson

Rotary, Lions Club, Chamber of Commerce, and other business groups	President or program chairperson
Business networking groups, such as LEADS	President or program chairperson
Local businesses	President, owner, or manager
Civic and professional organizations	President or program chairperson

Sample Text for Marketing Letter, Brochure, or Postcard

_____ is offering to present "Managing Conflict Creatively," an educational workshop, as a community service. In this workshop, participants will explore how to manage conflict in almost any situation. Through written exercises and group discussions, we will focus on common workplace situations where conflicts arise. As a result of attending this workshop, participants will learn new ways to resolve conflicts more productively and how to prevent them from happening in the first place.

_____ is a licensed _____ in private practice in _____. S/he specializes in _____ and _____. Call _____ today to schedule your group's **free** workshop. (_____) _____-_____.

Sample Text for Press Release

_____ Presents "Managing Conflict Creatively" Seminar

_____ is presenting a **free** workshop on how to manage conflict. The workshop is scheduled for _____, from _____ to _____ at ____. The workshop is limited to ____ participants and is open to the public.

According to _____, "The world has become increasingly stressful in recent years. Relationships are difficult to maintain and disagreements and conflicts are more common than ever. People skills have become more important than ever, especially the ability to manage conflict. This workshop provides an overview of some productive ways to deal with conflicts in almost any situation."

_____ is a licensed _____ in private practice in _____. S/he specializes in _____ and _____. For reservations, call _____ at (_____) _____-_____.

Exhibit 11.1   Presentation Outline

Managing Conflict Creatively

Topic	*Time Estimate*
I. Introduction	
A. Introduce yourself	1 minute
🕐 B. Ask group members to introduce themselves	10 minutes
C. State workshop goals	1 minute
II. Kinds of Conflicts	3 minutes
III. Common Ways of Dealing with Conflict	15 minutes
🕐 Three video examples	
IV. The Effects of Conflict on Relationships	15 minutes
🕐	
V. Factors That Affect Conflict Management	10 minutes
🕐	
VI. Conflict Resolution Skills	
🕐 A. Active listening skills	7–10 minutes
• Examples	
• Benefits	
🕐 B. Assertive communication skills	7–10 minutes
🕐 C. De-Escalation Skills	7–10 minutes
VII. Conflict Prevention Skills	10 minutes
🕐	
VIII. Conclusion	
Approximate Total Time	**54–95 minutes**

Exhibit 11.2   Presentation Script

Managing Conflict Creatively

Outline	Presenter's Comments	Activity
I-A. **Introduce Yourself**	My name is _____. I'm a licensed _____, with a _____. I specialize in working with _____. Many of my clients come to me with stories of conflict in their relationships both at home and at work. Conflict presents a problem for many people and adds tremendous stress to their lives. When I approached _____ about presenting a workshop on managing conflict creatively, his/her reaction was _____. So that is why we are here today.	Refer to your bio on the first page of the handouts. 1 minute.
I-B. **Group Intro** 🕐	I'd like to start things off by finding out a bit about each of you. Let's go around the room; introduce yourself and tell us something about yourself.	If the group is under 20 people, ask participants to introduce themselves. 10 minutes.
I-C. **Goals**	In this workshop, we will explore how to manage conflict in your everyday relationships. Through written exercises and group discussions, we will focus on where conflicts arise and how we typically deal with them. By the end of this workshop, you will have learned some new ways to resolve these conflicts more productively. You will also learn some ways to prevent conflicts from happening in the first place.	State goals. 1 minute.
II. **Kinds of Conflicts**	Let's start by identifying where conflicts happen. Think about the kinds of conflicts that happen in your daily life. What are some examples? You may wish to take notes on Handout 11.1.	Handout 11.1. 3 minutes.
🕐	**Look for answers like these:** • Disagreements over who should do what • Disagreements over how things should be done • Conflicts of personality and style	List suggestions on easel pad. If time is short, present info as a lecture.

11.5

Outline	Presenter's Comments	Activity
III. **Common Ways** **of Dealing with** **Conflict** 🕐	Now that we've identified some typical situations where conflict arises in your everyday lives, let's look at some examples of ways that people deal with them.	Present information. 15 minutes.
	First, let's look at two examples from movies you may have seen. In *Waiting to Exhale,* Angela Bassett's character deals with conflict like this. (*Show the scene where Angela Bassett's character torches her husband's car.*)	Show video. Lead discussion.
🕐	Here is another way of dealing with conflict. In *Alice in Wonderland,* Alice and her friends respond to conflict instigated by the Queen like this. (*Show the scene where Alice and the playing cards agree with everything the Queen says.*)	Show video. Lead discussion.
🕐	Here is a third way of dealing with conflict. In *Ordinary People,* Mary Tyler Moore plays Beth, a wife and mother who responds to conflict in her family like this. (*Show the scene where Beth [Mary Tyler Moore] has lunch with her husband Calvin [Donald Sutherland] as they are Christmas shopping at the mall.*) What are some other common ways of dealing with conflict? You may want to list these on Handout 11.1.	Show video. Lead discussion.
🕐	**Typical answers:** • Avoid the conflict. • Deny the conflict; wait until it goes away (like Beth). • Change the subject. • React emotionally: become aggressive, abusive, hysterical or frightening (like the Queen and Angela Bassett's character). • Find someone to blame. • Make excuses. • Delegate the situation to someone else. What is wrong with these ways of responding? **Target answer:** All of these responses are nonproductive. All of them are destructive, some physically. This is why learning to manage conflict is so important.	List responses on blank easel. If time is short, present info as a lecture.
IV. Effect on **Relationships**	Relationships have different aspects, like trust between people and the self-esteem of the individuals involved. When conflicts are handled well, what is the effect on each	List responses on Handout 11.1. 15 minutes.

of the workplace factors listed on Handout 11.1? And when conflicts are handled poorly, what is the effect?

🕐

Look for the following answers:

Relationship Factor	How It Is Affected When Conflict Is Handled Well	How It Is Affected When Conflict Is Handled Badly
Trust	Increases.	Decreases.
Teamwork	Improves.	Quality declines.
Morale	Improves.	Declines
Self-esteem	Increases.	Declines
Loyalty	Increases.	Declines
Respect for boss	Increases.	Declines.
Productivity	Increases.	Decreases.
Future behavior	People feel free to express differing viewpoints.	People avoid conflict and withhold their viewpoints to avoid negative consequences.

Typical answers.

If time is short, present info as a lecture.

V. Factors That Affect How People Manage Conflict

The skills involved in managing conflict are learned behaviors. None of us is born knowing how to deal with differences of opinion or arguments or turf wars. Some of the factors that affect how we behave in the face of conflict are:

1. Behavior learned in our families
2. Behavior learned from our role models
3. Status
4. Unwritten rules
5. Gender differences

These factors are listed on Handout 11.1. What are some examples of each of these factors? You may wish to note them on the handout.

Prelist these factors on easel pad.

10 minutes.

Note examples on Handout 11.1.

🕐

Offer your ideas if needed to move the discussion along:

- *Behavior learned in families.* In some families, conflict and confrontation are a communication style. In others, conflict always remains hidden.

- *Behavior learned from role models.* People who have had a teacher or boss who modeled effective conflict resolution skills are more likely to develop these skills themselves.

Encourage participants to come up with these answers.

If time is limited, present these ideas as a lecture.

11.7

Outline	Presenter's Comments	Activity

• *Status.*   People in higher-status positions usually feel freer to engage in conflict and are less likely to avoid confrontation.

• *Unwritten rules.*   Some groups encourage conflict; others have unwritten rules that it is to be contained or avoided.

• *Gender differences.*   Males are generally encouraged to be more confrontational than females.

VI.
Conflict Resolution Skills

No one is *born* knowing how to resolve conflicts. Conflict resolution is a set of skills that anyone can learn. These skills include:

1. Active listening
2. Assertive communication skills
3. Deescalation skills

Let's spend a moment exploring each of these three skills.

Activity: Present information. 30 minutes.

VI-A.
Active Listening

You may wish to take notes on Handout 11.2.

Active listening is a valuable skill for resolving conflicts because it enables you to demonstrate that you understand what another person is saying and how he or she is feeling about it. Active listening means restating, in your own words, what the other person has said.

Active listening is a way of checking whether your understanding is correct. It also demonstrates that you are listening and that you are interested and concerned. These all help resolve a situation where there are conflicting points of view.

Active listening responses have two components:

1. Naming the feeling that the other person is conveying
2. Stating the reason for the feeling

Activity: Take notes on Handout 11.2.

Active Listening Examples

Here are some examples of active listening statements:

Sounds like you're upset about what happened at work.

You're annoyed by my lateness, aren't you?

You sound really stumped about how to solve this problem.

It makes you angry when you find errors on Joe's paperwork.

Sounds like you're really worried about Wendy.

I get the feeling you're awfully busy right now.

Actively listening is *not* the same as agreement. It is a way of demonstrating that you intend to hear and understand another's point of view.

Active Listening Benefits

If a person uses active listening as part of his or her communication style at work, how would that be good for resolving conflicts—that is, what are the benefits?

Possible responses:

- It feels good when another person makes an effort to understand what you are thinking and feeling. It creates good feelings about the other person and makes you feel better about yourself.

- Restating what you've heard and checking for understanding promotes better communication and produces fewer misunderstandings.

- Responding with Active Listening has a calming effect in an emotional situation.

Lead discussion.

Please take a moment to try this yourself. You will find three work situations described on Handout 11.2. Write an active listening response for each one, making sure to include the two components we talked about.

Allow 3 minutes.

(Ask participants to read their responses.)

1. Your spouse says to you, "What happened to this house while I was gone? It looks like a bomb went off here."

   Sample response: "You sound annoyed that the house is a mess."

2. Your daughter comes home after you have spent the day painting the living room. She says, "How do you expect me to invite my friends over when this place looks like a place out of the sixties?"

   Sample response: "You seem pretty unhappy with the color I chose for this room."

3. Your neighbor says, "Your yard is making this neighborhood look like a trailer park."

   Sample response: "You seem pretty upset about the fact that I haven't been able to get these leaves raked yet."

If time is short, suggest that participants complete exercises later.

11.9

Outline	Presenter's Comments	Activity
VI-B. **Assertive Communication Skills**	Another skill that will help you manage conflict effectively is to be assertive (rather than aggressive or passive) in your communication. The DESC script (outlined by Sharon and Gordon Bower in *Asserting Yourself*) is a way to help you plan an assertive message. It is a tool for organizing your thoughts so you are less likely to forget what you want to say and how you want to say it. It helps minimize conflicts because it is straightforward and assertive, focusing on your view of the situation.	Present information.

The DESC message has four components: *describe, express, specify,* and *consequences.* This is what the four steps mean:

- *Describe* the problem or issue.
- *Express* your feelings about the situation.
- *Specify* what you want the other person to do. Be specific, including when you want the action completed.
- State the *consequences:* describe what you will do if the other person does not do what you are requesting.

This is an assertive alternative to saying, "Do it my way or you're grounded" or "You need to get this job done by noon."

🕐	Let's get some practice with this technique by completing the exercise on Handout 11.3.	Handout 11.3. Allow 3 minutes.
	Who would like to read their DESC Script for the first exercise?	If time is short, suggest that participants complete exercises later.
	(Ask different people to read their answers. Reinforce responses that are assertive; point out those that sound too threatening.)	
VI-C. **Deescalation Skills**	Everyone has been in an argument that has escalated. Before you know it, it's blown out of proportion. Let's think for a moment about some actions that will help you deescalate a conflict. In your experience, what actions put a stop to the defend/attack spiral? You may wish to list these on Handout 11.4.	Handout 11.4.

🕐	**Typical responses:** • Stick with "I" statements; avoid "you" statements. • Avoid name-calling and put-downs ("a reasonable person could see that . . ."). • Soften your tone. • Take a time-out ("Let's take a break and cool down").	If time is short, present as a lecture.

Outline	Presenter's Comments	Activity

- Acknowledge the other person's point of view (agreement is not necessary).
- Avoid defensive or hostile body language (rolling eyes, crossing arms in front of body, tapping foot).
- Be specific and factual; avoid generalities.

VII.
Conflict
Prevention
Skills

Now that we've talked about how to resolve a conflict, let's look at how to prevent conflicts from happening. Think of situations in your life where there don't seem to be many conflicts. What might be happening there? You may wish to note these on Handout 11.5.

Handout 11.5.

Lead discussion.

10 minutes.

Responses to look for:

- Bring issues out in the open before they become problems.
- Be aware of triggers and respond to them when you notice them.
- Have a process for resolving conflicts. Bring it up at a meeting and get agreement on what people should do in cases of differing viewpoints.
- Teach everyone conflict resolution skills and expect people to use them.

List ideas on easel.

If time is short, information may be presented as a lecture.

IX.
Conclusion

I hope you have enjoyed today's workshop. In the time remaining, I would be happy to answer any questions you may have.

Conclude the workshop.

Handout 11.1   Handling Conflicts

1. What kinds of conflicts typically occur in your everyday life?

2. What are some common ways of dealing with conflict?

3. What is the effect of each of these actions on the following relationship factors?

Relationship Factor	How Is This Factor Affected When Conflict Is Handled Well?	How Is This Factor Affected When Conflict Is Handled Badly?
Trust	_____	_____
Teamwork	_____	_____
Morale	_____	_____
Self-esteem	_____	_____
Loyalty	_____	_____
Respect	_____	_____
Productivity	_____	_____
Future behavior	_____	_____

4. These are some of the factors that affect how people manage conflict. Think of an example of each.

Behavior learned in our families: _____

Behavior learned from our role models: _____

Status: _____

A group's unwritten rules: _____

Gender differences: _____

Handout 11.2   Active Listening

Active listening is a valuable skill for managing conflict because

_____

An active listening response has two components:

1. _____

2. _____

Responding with active listening has these benefits:

1. _____

2. _____

3. _____

Write an active listening response to each of the following statements.

1. Your spouse says to you, "What happened to this house while I was gone? It looks like a bomb went off here."

   I could say: _____

   _____

   _____

2. Your daughter comes home after you have spent the day painting the living room. She says, "How do you expect me to invite my friends over when this place looks like a place out of the sixties?"

   I could say: _____

   _____

   _____

3. Your neighbor says, "Your yard is making this neighborhood look like a trailer park."

   I could say: _____

   _____

   _____

Handout 11.3   Assertive Communication Skills

The DESC Script

D _____

E _____

S _____

C _____

Situation 1.   Your son has taken your car to school today and has just come home 30 minutes late. This is the third time in two weeks that he has done this. His lateness has caused you to miss a doctor's appointment.

Describe: _____

Express: _____

Specify: _____

Consequences: _____

Situation 2.   Your daughter had some friends over last night. They were watching videos in your basement. This morning, you go down there to exercise, and you see that she did not clean up the mess they made.

Describe: _____

Express: _____

Specify: _____

Consequences: _____

Situation 3.   You are planning a weekend trip in July to attend a reunion of some of your college friends. Your husband knows that you have been planning this event for a long time. Today you find out that he has made plans to be gone the same weekend for an educational seminar. Now you will have to make arrangements for someone to care for your dog and teenager.

Describe: _____

Express: _____

Specify: _____

Consequences: _____

Source: Sharon and Gordon Bower, *Asserting Yourself* (New York: Addison-Wesley, 1976).

Handout 11.4   Conflict Deescalation

List actions that can help deescalate a conflict:

1. _____
   _____
   _____

2. _____
   _____
   _____

3. _____
   _____
   _____

4. _____
   _____
   _____

5. _____
   _____
   _____

6. _____
   _____
   _____

7. _____
   _____
   _____

Handout 11.5　Preventing Conflict

List ways to prevent conflicts from happening:

1. _____

_____

_____

2. _____

_____

_____

3. _____

_____

_____

4. _____

_____

_____

5. _____

_____

_____

6. _____

_____

_____

7. _____

_____

_____

Chapter 12

Managing the Emotional
Challenges of Caregiving

Presentation Synopsis

Few people are prepared for the responsibilities and tasks involved in caring for loved ones who are ill, elderly, or disabled. The success of the relationship between you and your loved one depends on several factors. One of the most important is how well you take care of yourself, empowering yourself to be there for the person you are caring for. In this workshop, you will learn some ways to care for yourself as you care for another.

This presentation is based, in part, on information drawn from the following books. I recommend that you review them as you prepare your presentation:

Berman, Claire. *Caring for Yourself while Caring for Your Aging Parents: How to Help, How to Survive.* New York: Henry Holt, 1996.

Booth, Cathy. "Taking Care of Our Aging Parents." *Time,* August 30, 1999.

Brandt, Avrene. *Caregiver's Reprieve: A Guide to Emotional Survival When You're Caring for Someone You Love.* San Luis Obispo, CA: Impact, 1998.

Greenwald, John. "Elder Care: Making the Right Choice." *Time,* August 30, 1999.

Haigler, David, Kathryn Mims, and Jack Nottingham. *Caring for You, Caring for Me: Education and Support for Caregivers.* Americus, GA: Rosalynn Carter Institute, Georgia Southwestern State University, 1998.

Jackson, Billie. *The Caregivers' Roller Coaster: A Practical Guide to Caregiving for the Frail Elderly.* Chicago: Loyola University Press, 1993.

Kübler-Ross, Elisabeth. *On Death and Dying.* New York: Scribners, 1977.

Time Requirements

This presentation runs from 1 to 2 hours, depending on the style of the presenter and the number of interactive activities used.

☐ **Clock symbol.** This means that the information is included for a longer seminar or workshop. Omit these sections for a shorter presentation. If time is limited, another way to shorten your presentation is to share the information in lecture format. However, keep in mind that it is often harder to engage and maintain the audience's interest with a pure lecture style. Unless you are a particularly dynamic speaker, you will probably want to keep at least a few of the exercises to enliven the presentation.

Video examples. Showing selected scenes from popular movies is one way to make your presentation more interesting. It creates some variety and interest and stimulates discussion. Consider selecting short scenes from videos such as *What Dreams May Come* and *Hilary and Jackie*. Suggestions for specific scenes are included in this outline, but you are encouraged to look for other examples on your own as you prepare for your presentation.

How to Use This Presentation

Possible Audiences	Whom to Contact
Adult education groups at churches and synagogues	Director of adult education programs
Caregiver support groups	Executive directors of residential care homes, intermediate care facilities and nursing homes
	Directors of educational programs at local hospitals
Women's civic and professional organizations	Director of educational programs

Sample Text for Marketing Letter, Brochure, or Postcard

Few people are prepared for the responsibilities and tasks involved in caring for loved ones who are ill, elderly, or disabled. The success of the relationship between you and your loved one depends on how well you take care of yourself, enabling you to be there for the person you are caring for. In this workshop, you will learn some ways to care for yourself as you care for another. Through written exercises and group discussion, participants develop personal strategies for managing the many stresses of caring for a family member who is sick, disabled, or elderly.

_____ is a licensed _____ in private practice in _____. S/he specializes in _____ and _____ Call _____ today to schedule your group's **free** workshop. (_____) _____-_____.

Sample Text for Press Release

_____ Presents "Managing the Emotional Challenges of Caregiving"

_____ is presenting a **free** workshop on how to create a life for yourself that reflects your personal values and life goals. The workshop is scheduled for _____, from _____ to _____ at _____. The workshop is limited to _____ participants and is open to the public. According to _____, "Few people are prepared for the responsibilities and tasks involved in caring for loved ones who are ill, elderly, or disabled. The success of the relationship between you and your loved one depends on how well you take care of yourself, enabling you to be there for the person you are caring for. In this workshop, you will learn some ways to care for yourself as you care for another."

_____ is a licensed _____ in private practice in _____ S/he specializes in _____ and _____. For reservations, call _____ at (_____) _____-_____.

Exhibit 12.1   Presentation Outline

Managing the Emotional Challenges of Caregiving

Topic	*Time Estimate*
I. **Introduction**	
A. Introduce yourself	1 minute
⏱ B. Ask group members to introduce themselves	10 minutes
C. State workshop goals	1 minute
II. **Facts about Caregiving**	3 minutes
III. **Caregiving Stages**	13 minutes
⏱ Video examples	20 minutes
IV. **Responding to Loss**	15 minutes
V. **Sources of Stress**	25 minutes
A. Geographic stress	
B. Financial stress	
C. Cultural expectations	
D. Family/relationship stress	
E. Physical stress	
F. Home alterations	
G. Social stress	
H. Emotional stress	
VI. **Signs of Burnout**	5 minutes
VII. **How to Prevent Burnout**	5 minutes
VIII. **Bill of Rights**	6 minutes
IX. **Conclusion**	
Approximate Total Time	**74–104 minutes**

Managing the Emotional Challenges of Caregiving

Outline	Presenter's Comments	Activity
I-A. **Introduce Yourself**	My name is _____. I'm a licensed _____, with a _____. I specialize in working with _____, and became interested in the effect that caring for a sick, disabled or elderly family member has on people about _____ ago, when _____ _____.	Refer to your bio on the first page of the handouts. 1 minute.
I-B. **Group Intro** ⏱	I'd like to begin today's workshop by finding out a bit about each of you. Let's go around the room and each of you give your name and tell us what brought you to this workshop.	If the group is under 20 people, ask participants to introduce themselves. 10 minutes.
I-C. **Goals**	Few people are prepared for the responsibilities and tasks involved in caring for loved ones who are ill, elderly, or disabled. The success of the relationship between you and your loved one depends on several factors. One of the most important is how well you take care of yourself, empowering yourself to be there for the person you are caring for. In this workshop, you will learn some ways to care for yourself as you care for another.	State goals. 1 minute.
II. **Facts about Caregiving**	You may wish to take notes on Handout 12.1. • There are 7 million caregivers in the United States. These are people who are responsible for the health and care of an aged or chronically ill loved one. • 70 to 80 percent of the elderly are cared for at home by their family members. This can mean a commitment of 10 to 20 years. According to *Time* magazine (August 30, 1999): • The current average life expectancy in the United States is 76 years. • 43 percent of today's senior citizens will use a nursing home during their lifetime. • In 1995, about 12 percent of the U.S. population was 65 or older. By 2030, that will rise to about 20 percent.	Handout 12.1. Present information. 3 minutes.

Outline	Presenter's Comments	Activity
III. Caregiving Stages	When a person becomes a caregiver to a member of his or her family, there are certain stages that the caregiver and the family pass through. Think about which stage you are in now: 1. Learning about what the patient needs. 2. Building a support team. 3. Relationships begin to change; roles begin to shift; losses become apparent. 4. People react to losses and changes; depression and other emotional reactions are common.	Present information. 3 minutes.
🕐	To illustrate how losses affect people, I'd like to show two scenes from recent movies. First, let's look at a scene from the 1998 movie *What Dreams May Come*. Robin Williams plays Christy, who is married to Annie (played by Annabella Sciorra). Their two children are tragically killed in an auto accident, and Annie becomes severely depressed and is hospitalized. Christy himself is later killed in another accident, and Annie takes her own life and is sent to hell. Toward the end of the movie, Christy (Robin) finds Annie in the Sea of Doubt and falls with her to Hell House. There he tries to connect with her so he can bring her to his paradise to live with him. *(Suggested scene: Christy says to Annie, "He pushed away the pain so hard he disconnected himself from the person he loved the most." You may also wish to show the scene on the grounds of the hospital where Christy tells Annie he is thinking of leaving her.)* How does this scene relate to your situation? Are you sometimes tempted to disconnect yourself from the person you are caring for? How do you behave when you are disconnected?	Show video scene. Lead discussion. 10 minutes.
🕐	Our second film scene is from the 1998 movie *Hilary and Jackie*. This is the true story of Jacqueline and Hilary du Pré, the gifted musical sisters who grew up in England in the 1950s. Written and produced as a tribute to Jackie, the story traces her rapid rise to international fame as a cellist, as well as the devastating effect fame had on her and those she loved. Jackie and her husband, the pianist and conductor Daniel Barenboim, traveled and performed around the world. Tragically, Jackie developed multiple sclerosis at the age of 26, ending her career. The disease progressed quickly and she died 14 years later.	Show video scene. Lead discussion. 10 minutes.

Outline	*Presenter's Comments*	*Activity*

(Suggested scene: Toward the end of the film, Jackie [in London] talks with Daniel [in Paris] on the telephone. It is apparent he has created a new family for himself while the disease destroys her body. In the next scene, she says, "When you play, everyone loves you. When you stop, they don't love you any longer.")

How does this scene relate to your situation? What effect has your loved one's illness or disability had on your family relationships?

What effect has your loved one's illness or disability had on your family?

Which caregiving stage are you in now?

What stage has been the most difficult?

Lead discussion of each question separately. Encourage participants to respond as time allows.

10 minutes.

IV. Responding to Loss

Having a person in your family who is disabled, ill or who cannot take care of him- or herself is an experience of loss. Most people find it helpful to understand how loss affects us, since understanding it makes it easier to handle. Let's take a moment to discuss this now.

Present information.

In her work on death and dying, Elisabeth Kübler-Ross outlined five stages of reacting to loss. You will find these listed on Handout 12.2. These responses apply not only to the loss of a person through death, but to any kind of loss, including the loss of a way of life, the loss of abilities, and so on.

Handout 12.2.

15 minutes.

The changes you see in your loved one and the changes that are occurring in your life may lead you to respond in the following ways:

1. *Denial.* The first reaction to loss is often to deny it. You may feel numb, weak, tired, overwhelmed, anxious, or withdrawn. You may also keep yourself too busy to feel the pain of your situation.

    Denial is understandable because by rejecting or blocking painful feelings and thoughts, you don't have to face what is happening to the person you care about and to your way of life.

    Another form of denial is to anesthetize oneself. This can take the form of becoming so immersed in the details of caregiving that one doesn't have time to feel. It can also mean self-medicating with drugs or alcohol. When people stay stuck in this stage, it is difficult to move on, because when the anesthetic (work, drugs, or alcohol) wears off, the pain remains. If the pain is not experienced, it is impossible to move on.

How have you experienced denial in your situation?

2. *Anger.* As the reality of your situation sinks in, you can expect to become angry. You may feel anger toward the person you are caring for, anger toward God, or toward your family members, the doctors, or others.

How have you experienced anger in your situation?

3. *Bargaining.* It is not unusual to ask God to make some kind of bargain to make the loss go away, such as "Maybe if I go to church every Sunday, George will recover" or a similar request.

How have you experienced bargaining in your situation?

4. *Depression.* Many people report feeling deep sadness, disturbed sleep and eating patterns, thoughts of suicide, or excessive crying.

How have you experienced depression in your situation?

5. *Acceptance.* Eventually, you will begin to accept what has happened and even look for the lessons of the experience.

How have you experienced acceptance?

Seeing your loved one change is an experience of loss and involves grief. Kübler-Ross said that the grieving process involves experiencing all five stages, although not always in this order. She also said that people often cycle back and forth through the stages before coming to the stage of acceptance.

V.
Sources of
Stress

Caring for someone who is sick or disabled causes tremendous stress. We are going to look at eight sources of stress (listed on Handout 12.3):

1. Geographic stress: caregiving from a distance
2. Financial stress
3. Cultural expectations
4. Family/relationship stress
5. Physical stress

Present information.

Handout 12.3.

25 minutes.

6. Home alterations
7. Social stress
8. Emotional stress

V-A.
Geographic
Stress

Geographic stress: In most families, people are spread out across the country and are not always available to help with caring for a sick or elderly person. If you live far away from someone who requires care and want to participate as much as you can, here are some ideas suggested by Billie Jackson in her book *The Caregivers' Roller Coaster:*

Present information.

Ask for examples of each as time allows.

- Contribute money for weekly maid service.
- Contribute money for a sitter to provide a break for the primary caregiver.
- Pay for a trip to the beauty salon for the primary caregiver and/or the patient.
- Pay for medical equipment that is not covered by insurance.
- Send special treats for the primary caregiver as a way of expressing appreciation for the work he or she is doing.
- Write often and express appreciation for the work being done.
- Call regularly and encourage the caregiver to vent his or her feelings and concerns. Be a sympathetic listener.

V-B.
Financial
Stress

Financial stress is very common in families where someone requires an excessive amount of care. What are some examples of what can happen?

Answers to look for:

- Caregivers are often required to spend their own money to cover expenses that are not covered by insurance or medicare.

- Less-involved family members may not realize how expensive various required items are and may resist helping to pay for them.

- The primary caregiver may be required to work less, find a less demanding kind of work (which pays less), or stop working altogether in order to care for the patient.

V-C.
Cultural
Expectations

Cultural expectations: In some cultures, daughters are expected to care for parents, and in others it is not acceptable to place relatives in nursing homes. How has your ethnic or cultural background affected your experience of being a caregiver?

Outline	Presenter's Comments	Activity
V-D. **Family/** **Relationship** **Stress**	*Family/relationship stress:* In addition to the financial stress, all of these factors create tremendous stress on the relationships among family members and may lead to additional turmoil if they are not openly discussed and resolved.	
V-E. **Physical** **Stress**	*Physical stress:* Caring for an impaired person is physically stressful. Activities like cleaning, doing the laundry, shopping, and making meals can be exhausting, especially when taken on in addition to the responsibilities of your own life. Lifting and moving people with limited mobility is not only tiring, but also can result in injury (to yourself or the patient).	
V-F. **Home** **Alterations**	*Home alterations:* If the patient continues to live at home, you may need to make alterations, such as building ramps or railings. Everyone in the home will have to adjust. If the patient cannot stay in the home, other arrangements must be made. This could mean moving in with a friend or relative or looking for special housing (residential care homes, intermediate care facilities, nursing homes, etc.).	
V-G. **Social Stress**	*Social stress:* Providing personal care 24 hours a day can cause social stress by isolating the primary caregiver from family and friends. You may be too tired to have an evening out weekly or even monthly, or you may not have anyone else to take over. This can result in a buildup of anger and resentment toward the person receiving the care.	
V-H. **Emotional** **Stress**	*Emotional stress:* All of these factors inevitably result in tremendous emotional stress. It is common to feel any of the following: • Anger and resentment about the magnitude of work, feelings of deprivation and isolation • Anxiety and frustration about unresolved conflicts between family members • Resentment about the loss of your privacy • Frustration over your inability to control what is happening to your family member • Sadness as the patient's health worsens • Fantasies about placing the patient in an institution or even wishing he or she would die • Guilt feelings about having such thoughts • Denial that you have such thoughts	

Outline	Presenter's Comments	Activity
VI. **Signs of** **Burnout**	Along with the negative emotions, you probably feel love for your family member and satisfaction from making a difference in his or her life.	
	Such conflicting emotions may cause guilt and stress. The stresses we talked about earlier add to all of this, and many caregivers become so overwhelmed that they burn out.	
	How do you know if the stress is becoming too much for you? Handout 12.4 is a list of 24 signs that you need help. Take a moment to look through these and identify those that are now problems for you or may be potential problems.	Handout 12.4. Present information. Participants read handout and identify own issues.
	Who would like to share what you have identified for yourself?	Lead discussion. 5 minutes.
VII. **How to** **Prevent** **Burnout**	There are many resources that can help caregivers deal with these stresses and prevent burnout. Handout 12.5 lists 20 ideas; let's look at each one and add yours.	Handout 12.5. Read through handout. Add own ideas. Lead short discussion. 5 minutes.
VIII. **Bill of Rights**	Handout 12.6 is a bill of rights for caregivers. As you read each item on this list, note specifically how it applies to you. Take a few minutes to go through this and make some notes.	Handout 12.6. Individual exercise.
	Which of the items on the list were the most important to you?	Lead discussion. 6 minutes.
IX. **Conclusion**	I hope you have enjoyed today's workshop. In the time remaining, I would be happy to answer any questions you may have.	Conclude the workshop.

Handout 12.1　Facts about Caregiving

Facts about Caregiving

1. _____
2. _____
3. _____
4. _____
5. _____

Stages of Caregiving

1. _____
2. _____
3. _____
4. _____

What effect has your loved one's illness or disability had on your family? _____
_____
_____

Which caregiving stage are you in now? _____
_____

What stage has been the most difficult? _____
_____

Handout 12.2   The Five Stages of Grief Recovery

1. Denial

    _____

    _____

2. Anger

    _____

    _____

3. Bargaining

    _____

    _____

4. Depression

    _____

    _____

5. Acceptance

    _____

    _____

Source: Adapted and reprinted with the permission of Simon & Schuster from *On Death and Dying* by Elisabeth Kübler-Ross. Copyright © 1969 by Elisabeth Kübler-Ross.

Handout 12.3   Sources of Stress

1. Geographic stress

    _____

    _____

    _____

    _____

    _____

2. Financial stress

    _____

    _____

    _____

    _____

    _____

3. Cultural expectations

    _____

    _____

    _____

    _____

    _____

4. Family/relationship stress

    _____

    _____

    _____

    _____

5. Physical stress

_____
_____
_____
_____
_____

6. Home alterations

_____
_____
_____
_____
_____

7. Social stress

_____
_____
_____
_____
_____

8. Emotional stress

_____
_____
_____
_____
_____

Handout 12.4   Signs That a Caregiver Needs Help

1. You don't get out much anymore.

2. You argue with the person you care for.

3. You have conflicts with other family members.

4. You abuse drugs, alcohol, or medications.

5. Your appetite has changed.

6. You isolate yourself from others.

7. You behave in a compulsive manner or are overly focused on minor details.

8. You behave rudely toward others.

9. You feel listless; you lack energy.

10. You feel more angry, anxious, or worried than usual.

11. You have a difficult time controlling your emotions.

12. You cry frequently.

13. You have a hard time concentrating.

14. You have physical symptoms of anxiety, such as an upset stomach, headaches, or racing heart.

15. You often forget things.

16. You are clumsy or accident-prone.

17. You have self-destructive or suicidal thoughts.

18. You have little or no interest in things that you used to enjoy.

19. You sleep more or less than usual.

20. You worry excessively (about money; about your ability to provide proper care).

21. You never seem to get enough rest.

22. You don't have enough time for yourself.

23. You don't have time to be with other family members besides the person you care for.

24. You feel guilty about your situation.

Signs that I should address: _____

_____

_____

_____

Handout 12.5   Caregiver Survival Ideas

1. Ask your family and friends for all kinds of help. They may be able to contribute time, money, or knowledge.

2. Check out adult day care facilities. They provide many kinds of services such as nursing, meals, transportation, and help from social workers.

3. Arrange for meals to be delivered. Many organizations offer meal delivery programs.

4. Hire a home health aide. They can help with bathing, feeding, dressing, and giving medication, and may do light household tasks.

5. Look into homemaker services. They can help with shopping, cooking, doing laundry, cleaning the house, and taking patients to doctor's appointments.

6. Learn about services that provide transportation to and from doctor's appointments and other places.

7. Investigate resources available in your community *before* you need them.

8. Look for all the support you can find. Be on the lookout for individuals and groups that offer emotional, social, physical, and financial support.

9. Find out about skilled nursing services. They offer professional help with specific medical problems.

10. Find out what is available through local hospital supply services. They rent and sell medical supplies and equipment such as canes, walkers, hospital beds, and bath chairs.

11. Check out social day care services. They provide recreational activities, social work services, hot meals, transportation and some health services.

12. Keep the lines of communication open with your family and friends. When the stress increases and miscommunication happens, bring it out in the open immediately.

13. Take care of yourself. Eat well, exercise, and take a break when you need to.

14. Look into respite care services. They provide substitute caregivers, giving you the relief you need.

15. Stay involved in things that interest you. Work to maintain a sense of balance in your life.

16. Be realistic about what you can get done. Recognize what you can and cannot accomplish, set your priorities, and act accordingly.

17. Don't wait for friends and family members to come forward and offer to help. You may have to ask them for what you need.

Add your own ideas:

_____

_____

_____

_____

Handout 12.6 Caregiver Bill of Rights

As a caregiver, you have the right to:

1. Ask for outside help even though friends or family members may object. It is important to understand that your strength and stamina are limited.

    What this means to me: _____

    _____

    _____

    _____

    _____

2. Take pride in what you are doing. Acknowledge your hard work and perseverance in meeting the patient's needs.

    What this means to me: _____

    _____

    _____

    _____

    _____

3. Maintain the parts of your own life that do not involve the person you care for, just as you would if he or she were well. You have the right to do some things just for yourself.

    What this means to me: _____

    _____

    _____

    _____

    _____

4. Do not let anyone manipulate you with emotions.

    What this means to me: _____

    _____

    _____

    _____

    _____

5. Express anger, sadness, depression, and other feelings in appropriate ways.

What this means to me: _____

_____

_____

_____

_____

6. Accept people's gratitude for the work you do for the patient.

What this means to me: _____

_____

_____

_____

_____

7. Take good care of yourself. This is not selfishness. It will help you take better care of the patient.

What this means to me: _____

_____

_____

_____

_____

8. Create a life for yourself in the future, planning for the time when the patient will no longer need your full-time help.

What this means to me: _____

_____

_____

_____

_____

Chapter 13

Parenting Your Teenager

Presentation Synopsis

This presentation explores stages of adolescent development; ways to maintain communication with your teen; ideas for preventing high-risk behavior, addressing sexuality issues, and recognizing and responding to teen depression and eating disorders; and suggestions for building your teen's self-esteem.

This workshop contains references to information presented in the following books. You may wish to review them as you prepare your presentation:

Ames, Louise Bates, Frances L. Ilg, and Sidney M. Baker. *Your Ten- to Fourteen-Year-Old.* New York: Dell Trade Paperbacks, 1988.

Bell, Ruth. *Changing Bodies, Changing Selves,* 3rd ed. New York: Times Books, 1998.

Kelly, Kate. *The Complete Idiot's Guide to Parenting a Teenager.* New York: Alpha Books, 1996.

Riera, Michael. *Uncommon Sense for Parents with Teenagers.* Berkeley, CA: Celestial Arts, 1995.

Slap, Gail, and Martha Jablow. *Teenage Health Care.* New York: Simon & Schuster, 1994.

Time Requirements

This presentation runs from 1 to 1½ hours, depending on the style of the presenter.

How to Use This Presentation

Possible Audiences	**Whom to Contact**
Adult education groups at churches and synagogues	Director of adult education programs
PTO/PTA	PTO/PTA president
Civic and professional organizations	Director of educational programs

Sample Text for Marketing Letter, Brochure, or Postcard

Being the parent of a teenager sometimes feels like riding a bucking bronco. If your members have teens, they will appreciate attending this workshop. "Parenting Your Teenager" is a free workshop that explores several topics that are important to the parents of today's teens: stages of adolescent development; ways to maintain communication with your teen; ideas for preventing high-risk behavior, addressing sexuality issues, and recognizing and responding to teen depression and eating disorders; and suggestions for building your teen's self-esteem.

_____ is a licensed _____ in private practice in _____. S/he specializes in _____ and _____. Call _____ today to schedule your group's **free** workshop. (_____) _____-_____.

Sample Text for Press Release

Free Workshop for Parents of Teens

_____ is presenting "Parenting Your Teenager," a workshop designed for people raising today's adolescents. The presentation is scheduled for _____ at _____ in the _____.

The workshop will be lead by _____, who says, "Being the parent of a teenager sometimes feels like riding a bucking bronco. In this workshop, we will explore several topics that are important to the parents of today's teens: stages of adolescent development; ways to maintain communication with your teen; ideas for preventing high-risk behavior, addressing sexuality issues, and recognizing and responding to teen depression and eating disorders; and suggestions for building your teen's self-esteem."

_____ is a licensed _____ in private practice in _____. S/he specializes in _____ and _____. For reservations, call _____ at (_____) _____-_____.

Exhibit 13.1   Presentation Outline

Parenting Your Teenager

Topic	*Time Estimate*
I. **Introduction**	
A. Introduce yourself	1 minute
🕐 B. Ask group members to introduce themselves	10 minutes
C. State workshop goals	1 minute
II. **Stages of Development**	7 minutes
A. Physical	
B. Psychological	
C. Social	
D. Sexual	
E. Intellectual	
III. **How to Maintain Communication**	11 minutes
IV. **Preventing High-Risk Behavior**	7 minutes
V. **Characteristics of Effective Families**	7 minutes
VI. **Preventing Teen Substance Abuse**	5 minutes
VII. **Sexuality**	12 minutes
VIII. **Teen Depression**	8 minutes
IX. **Eating Disorders**	7 minutes
X. **How to Build Your Teen's Self-Esteem**	9 minutes
XI. **Conclusion**	
Approximate Total Time	**75–85 minutes**

Exhibit 13.2 Presentation Script

Parenting Your Teenager

Outline	Presenter's Comments	Activity
I-A. **Introduce Yourself**	My name is _____. I'm a licensed _____, with a _____. I specialize in working with _____ and _____. About ____ years ago, I became interested in the issues that single parents face. I started noticing that _____ _____.	Refer to your bio on the first page of the handouts. 1 minute.
I-B. **Group Intro** ⏰	I'd like to begin today's workshop by finding out a bit about each of you. Let's go around the room and each of you give your name and tell us what brings you to this workshop.	If the group is under 20 people, ask participants to introduce themselves. 10 minutes.
I-C. **Goals**	This presentation will explore ways that parents can successfully navigate the teen years. While it will not be easy, there are many things that parents can do to minimize problems and maximize family cohesiveness.	State goals. 1 minute.
II. **Developmental Tasks**	Adolescence is a process that involves a series of developmental tasks. When you think of all the things a person must accomplish during the years between 12 and 18, you can see that it's a very busy and important time. It's no wonder that a person is difficult to be around, with all of these tasks to accomplish. Let's take a look at them now. According to Gail Slap and Martha Jablow in their 1994 book *Teenage Health Care,* adolescents face quite a few developmental tasks. They could be divided into the categories you see listed on Handout 13.1—physical, emotional, social, sexual and intellectual. Let's see what each category includes. Please add your own ideas to each of these categories as we discuss them.	Handout 13.1. Present information. 7 minutes.
II-A. **Physical**	1. The *physical* changes that take place in adolescence are enormous. According to Slap and Jablow, "puberty affects virtually every tissue of the body" (page 14). They cite the following facts: • 40 percent of a person's adult weight and 25 percent of height are attained during the teen years.	

- Boys' hearts double in weight during puberty.

- Teens experience sexual maturation, which involves the development of breasts and genitals.

- Boys' voices change and they grow facial hair.

- Many teens have problems with acne.

II-B.
Psychological

2. The *psychological* changes that take place in adolescence revolve around becoming an autonomous person. To prepare for adulthood, the adolescent must make the transition from dependency to independence. In early adolescence, the child begins to withdraw from the family and resist parents' guidance and input, placing more importance on his or her peer group. Achieving autonomy is a necessary task but is the source of plenty of conflict.

II-C.
Social

3. The *social* changes that teens experience include the following:

- Learning to relate to other people
- Finding one's place in the group
- Learning responsible behavior
- Developing a system of values that will carry the adolescent successfully into adulthood

II-D.
Sexual

4. The *sexual* changes of adolescence are immense. As teenagers mature physically and become interested in others in a sexual way, they must learn:

- To be comfortable with their own bodies
- To take care of their sexual health
- To relate to others in a sexual way
- To deal with sexual feelings
- To make choices about sexual behavior

II-E.
Intellectual

5. The *intellectual* changes that take place in adolescence include:

- Learning to think abstractly
- Thinking about the future

III.
How to
Maintain
Communication

Why is it critical to maintain communication with your teen?

Lead discussion.

1 minute.

Answers to look for:

Even though teens need to separate from their parents during adolescence, they also need to know that the safety net of home and family is always there for them. If the lines

Outline	Presenter's Comments	Activity

of communication are shut down, they are not yet capable of surviving emotionally; they need support and input.

Let's take a look at a few guidelines for keeping the lines of communication open between parents and teenager. You may wish to make some notes on Handout 13.2.

Handout 13.2.

Present information.

10 minutes.

Don't

- Lecture your teen, offering little chance for him or her to respond.

- Behave in authoritarian manner ("You'll do it my way because I said so.").

- Begin a conversation with an accusation ("Mr. Jones said he saw you smoking.").

- Raise your voice or lose your temper. When you do, apologize later.

- Nag. It never works and only creates ill feelings.

- Criticize. Unless the issue involves behavior that is unsafe, unethical, or illegal, keep your opinions to yourself.

What would you like to add to this list?

Do

- Pay attention to the trivial as well as the important. If you are a good listener, your teen will be more likely to talk to you.

- When your teen talks to you, pay attention. Don't be doing something else.

- If you can't pay attention right at the moment, explain why and say how important it is. Ask if you can talk about the issue at a specific later time.

- Ask questions for clarification, but be sensitive to sounding as if you are being critical. If your teen perceives your questions as criticism, stop asking them.

- Expect your teen to change his or her mind frequently. Avoid commenting on the inconsistencies.

- Express interest and support in your teen's activities.

- Accept his or her opinions, even if you don't agree with them.

What would you like to add to this list?

Lead discussion

Outline	Presenter's Comments	Activity
IV. Preventing High-Risk Behavior	All parents fear their teens becoming involved in high-risk behaviors such as drinking, smoking, and sexual activity. There are some very specific things you can do to minimize your teen's need to act out. Here are some tips for preventing high-risk behavior (you may want to write them down on Handout 13.3):	Handout 13.3. Present information. 7 minutes.

- Be a part of your teen's life. If possible, be present when he or she is likely to be home.

- Be approachable. State that he or she can talk openly to you at any time.

- Be specific about what kind of behavior you expect and what is unacceptable.

- Keep harmful substances out of the house. This includes cigarettes, drugs and alcohol. When teens have access to these items, they are more likely to use them.

- Expect good things from your teen. Teens who know their parents expect the best have higher emotional well-being.

- Encourage your teen to become involved in school activities. Those who are involved at school engage in fewer high-risk behaviors.

What would you like to add to this list?

Lead discussion.

Outline	Presenter's Comments	Activity
V. Characteristics of Effective Families	Both research and common sense indicate that children who grow up in families that are emotionally healthy have a better chance at succeeding in the world when they become adults. These children are also more likely to have fewer problems during adolescence.	Handout 13.4. Present information. 7 minutes.

Let's talk about what these emotionally healthy families are like. You may wish to write these characteristics down on Handout 13.4.

1. There are guidelines and expectations for family members' behavior.

2. Family members are encouraged to express their opinions. Different points of view are encouraged.

3. All members are treated with respect and taken seriously.

4. There is a sense of emotional connection.

5. There is an atmosphere of caring and love in the family.

6. There is a group identity or sense of "we-ness."

Outline	Presenter's Comments	Activity

7. Family members enjoy doing things together.

8. People are flexible; there is a feeling of going with the flow.

What would you like to add to this list?   Lead discussion.

Now let's look at some of the characteristics of less effective families:

1. The husband and wife argue and treat each other disrespectfully.

2. The parents have emotional problems that prevent them from engaging with the children or with each other.

3. The children are controlled with punishment.

4. Self-esteem is not maintained or enhanced.

5. Only one parent is responsible for carrying out parenting responsibilities.

6. Family members abuse alcohol or drugs.

What would you like to add to this list?   Lead discussion.

VI. Preventing Teen Substance Abuse

Now let's talk about some of the risks that teens face. First, let's look at drugs and alcohol. Kate Kelly's *The Complete Idiot's Guide to Parenting a Teenager* lists seven ways to help your teen stay away from drugs and alcohol (you may list them on Handout 13.5):

Handout 13.5.
Present information.
5 minutes.

1. State your expectations clearly.

2. Pay attention to where your teen is.

3. When your teen leaves home, ask him or her to tell you where he or she is going. Feel free to ask for specifics.

4. If your teen says he or she is going one place but actually goes somewhere else, consider restricting his or her freedom for awhile.

5. Maintain communication with your teen and build rapport.

6. Remember that your teen is innocent until proven guilty. When you hear that he or she was at a party where liquor was consumed, ask him or her about it without being confrontational. For example, "Someone told me that you were at a party on Saturday and that kids were drinking beer. What can you tell me about it?" Stay open

to the possibility that there is a reasonable explanation for the story. If the story is true, this gives him or her the opening to tell you about it.

7. Build relationships with other parents and agree on the rules. If none of the kids in the group have complete freedom, there will be less peer pressure and more safety.

What would you like to add to this list?

Lead discussion.

**VII.
Sexuality**

Teens are having sex earlier and in greater numbers now than ever before. How do you feel about that?

Lead discussion.
2 minutes.

Author Kate Kelly says that the first thing to do when thinking about sex and your teen is to explore your own feelings and beliefs about the subject. Have you clarified for yourself and talked with your partner about the following questions?

- Is it okay to have premarital sex during college?

- If having sex at 18 is okay, what about 16?

- Is it okay to have sex without protection?

- Are the answers to these questions the same for both boys and girls?

Most people would agree that having sex too early is problematic because most teens are not emotionally prepared to handle the consequences. The role that a parent plays in a teen's sexual life is very important.

There are several factors that tend to make it less likely that your teen will have sex too early (you may list these on Handout 13.6):

Handout 13.6.
Present information.
10 minutes.

1. Making the decision to save sex for marriage

2. Having parents who disapprove of contraception by teenagers who are not married

3. Having a strong sense of self-esteem

4. Feeling accepted at school

5. Feeling part of one's family

6. Having appropriate parental supervision

7. Participating in activities at a church or synagogue

These factors that tend to encourage teens to be sexually active:

Outline	Presenter's Comments	Activity

1. Having low self-esteem

2. Having a poor relationship with one's parents

3. Having a lack of parental supervision

4. Seeming older than one's peers

5. Having a long-term romantic relationship

6. Using alcohol, drugs, or tobacco

7. Having poor school performance

8. Having parents who tolerate sexual activity

9. Coming from a family that lacks religious or spiritual focus

VIII.
Teen
Depression

Teens are known for their mood swings. Feeling sad or blue is common. But when should a parent become concerned about a teen's moods? Depression is different from the blues because it lasts longer and seems more intense. Clinical depression is an illness that can lead to very serious problems with lifelong implications. Some of the warning signs are listed on Handout 13.7. (*Read through warning signs; ask if anyone has any questions.*)

Handout 13.7.

Present information.

8 minutes.

If you think your teen's mood may be depression, here are some things you can do about it:

● Talk to your teen about how he or she is feeling. Help your teen get it off his or her chest. Encourage your teen to think of solutions to what is bothering him or her.

● Encourage physical activity.

● Check in with him or her more often than usual.

● If these steps don't help, and the problem seems serious, call a school counselor, teacher, or physician. Ask for a referral to a qualified, licensed professional who specializes in working with adolescents who have emotional problems.

IX.
Eating
Disorders

Eating disorders affect more girls than boys during adolescence. They are emotional disorders that require the intervention of a health professional before they become life-threatening. If you think your teen suffers from either anorexia or bulimia, do not hesitate to seek the advice of your physician. Early treatment greatly enhances the chances of recovery. In *The Complete Idiot's Guide to Parenting*

Handout 13.8.

Present information.

7 minutes.

13.11

Outline	*Presenter's Comments*	*Activity*

Teenagers, author Kelly lists the following warning signs for *anorexia* (you may list these on Handout 13.8):

1. Losing 25 percent of normal body weight without being on a diet

2. Having a distorted body image; complaining of being fat even though he or she is thin

3. Continuing to diet even when he or she is thin

4. Having a fear of gaining weight

5. Stopping monthly menstrual periods (amenorrhea), in girls

6. Being preoccupied with food, calories, cooking, and so on.

7. Exercising compulsively

8. Bingeing and purging

The warning signs for *bulimia* include the following:

1. Bingeing or eating uncontrollably, often in secret

2. Purging by strict dieting, fasting, vigorous exercise, vomiting, or abusing laxatives or diuretics

3. Using the bathroom frequently after meals

4. Having a preoccupation with body weight

5. Exhibiting depression or mood swings

6. Having irregular periods

7. Having dental problems, swollen cheek glands, or bloating

What to do: If you think your teen suffers from either anorexia or bulimia, do not hesitate to seek the advice of your physician. Early treatment greatly enhances the chances of recovery.

X.
How to Build Your Teen's Self-Esteem

Why is self-esteem so critical, especially during the teen years?

Lead discussion.
2 minutes.

Suggested answers:

- Our self-esteem is a critical factor in how each of us directs our life.

- How we feel about ourselves drives the choices we make, how we feel, how we respond to events, and just about everything we do.

- When we have strong self-esteem, we make positive choices based on what is best for us and those we care about.

- When our self-esteem is weak, we tend to make choices based on what others think and want.

You can help your teen build and maintain his or her self-esteem in the following ways (you may list these on Handout 13.9):

Handout 13.9.

Present information.

7 minutes.

- Listen to what your teen is saying to you, in words and actions.

- Ask your teen's opinion about things and accept it.

- Ask why he or she thinks what he or she does.

- Remind yourself that your teen needs to differentiate him- or herself from you. That is your teen's job as an adolescent, and it is healthy. Allow your teen to do it.

- Let your teen know that you love him or her.

- Let your teen know that you will always be there for him or her.

- Give your teen permission to explore ideas.

- Don't be threatened when your teen expresses him- or herself.

- Encourage your teen to express his or her feelings appropriately.

What would you add to this list?

**XI.
Conclusion**

I hope you have enjoyed today's workshop. In the time remaining, I would be happy to answer any questions you may have.

Conclude the workshop.

Handout 13.1   Adolescent Development

Physical _____
_____
_____
_____
_____

Psychological _____
_____
_____
_____
_____

Social _____
_____
_____
_____
_____

Sexual _____
_____
_____
_____
_____

Intellectual _____
_____
_____
_____
_____

Handout 13.2   How to Maintain Communication with Your Teen

Don't

1. _____
2. _____
3. _____
4. _____
5. _____
6. _____
7. _____
8. _____
9. _____
10. _____

Do

1. _____
2. _____
3. _____
4. _____
5. _____
6. _____
7. _____
8. _____
9. _____
10. _____

Handout 13.3   Preventing High-Risk Behavior

1. _____

2. _____

3. _____

4. _____

5. _____

6. _____

7. _____

8. _____

9. _____

10. _____

Handout 13.4   Characteristics of Effective Families

High-functioning families:

1. _____

2. _____

3. _____

4. _____

5. _____

6. _____

7. _____

8. _____

Low-functioning families:

1. _____

2. _____

3. _____

4. _____

5. _____

6. _____

Handout 13.5   Drugs and Alcohol

How to reduce the risks:

1. _____

2. _____

3. _____

4. _____

5. _____

6. _____

7. _____

Handout 13.6   Sexuality

Factors that discourage sexual activity:

1. _____

2. _____

3. _____

4. _____

5. _____

6. _____

7. _____

Factors that encourage sexual activity:

1. _____

2. _____

3. _____

4. _____

5. _____

6. _____

7. _____

8. _____

9. _____

Handout 13.7   Depression

Signs that it's more than just the blues:

1. A change in eating or sleeping habits

2. A loss of interest in friends or hobbies

3. Suddenly not caring for pets or prized possessions

4. A sudden change in school grades

5. Complaints of unusual stress

6. Withdrawal

7. A lack of interest in appearance

8. Feeling hopeless or full of self-hate

9. Feeling numb, uninterested, and listless

10. Loss of energy

11. Talking or thinking about death and dying

What to do about it:

1. _____

2. _____

3. _____

4. _____

Source: Ruth Bell, *Changing Bodies, Changing Selves,* 3rd ed. (New York: Times Books, 1998).

Handout 13.8 Eating Disorders

Signs of anorexia:

1. _____

2. _____

3. _____

4. _____

5. _____

6. _____

7. _____

8. _____

Signs of bulimia:

1. _____

2. _____

3. _____

4. _____

5. _____

6. _____

7. _____

What to do about it: _____

_____

_____

_____

_____

Handout 13.9   How to Build Your Teen's Self-Esteem

1. _____

2. _____

3. _____

4. _____

5. _____

6. _____

7. _____

About the Disk

Introduction

The forms on the enclosed disk are saved in Microsoft Word for Windows version 7.0. In order to use the forms, you will need to have word processing software capable of reading Microsoft Word for Windows version 7.0 files.

System Requirements

- IBM PC or compatible computer
- 3.5-inch floppy disk drive
- Windows 95 or later
- Microsoft Word for Windows version 7.0 (including the Microsoft converter*) or later or other word processing software capable of reading Microsoft Word for Windows 7.0 files.

How to Install the Files onto Your Computer

To install the files, follow these instructions:

1. Insert the enclosed disk into the floppy disk drive of your computer.
2. From the Start menu, choose **Run.**
3. Type **A:\SETUP** and press **OK.**
4. The opening screen of the installation program will appear. Press **OK** to continue.
5. The default destination directory is C:\MARRIAGE. If you wish to change the default destination, you may do so now.
6. Press **OK** to continue. The installation program will copy all files to your hard drive in the C:\MARRIAGE or user-designated directory.

Note: Many popular word processing programs are capable of reading Microsoft Word for Windows 7.0 files. However, users should be aware that a slight amount of formatting might be lost when using a program other than Microsoft Word. If your word processor cannot read Microsoft Word for Windows 7.0 files, unformatted text files have been provided in the TXT directory on the floppy disk.

---

* Word 7.0 needs the Microsoft converter file installed in order to view and edit all enclosed files. If you have trouble viewing the files, download the free converter from the Microsoft web site. The URL for the converter is http://officeupdate.microsoft.com/downloadDetails/wd97cnv.htm.

Microsoft also has a viewer that can be downloaded, which allows you to view but not edit documents. This viewer can be downloaded at http://officeupdate.microsoft.com/downloadDetails/wd97vwr32.htm.

Using the Files

LOADING FILES

To use the word processing files, launch your word processing program. Select **File, Open** from the pull-down menu. Select the appropriate drive and directory. If you installed the files to the default directory, the files will be located in the C:\MARRIAGE directory. A list of files should appear. If you do not see a list of files in the directory, you need to select **WORD DOCUMENT(*.DOC)** under **Files of Type.** Double-click on the file you want to open. Edit the file according to your needs.

PRINTING FILES

If you want to print the files, select **File, Print** from the pull-down menu.

SAVING FILES

When you have finished editing a file, you should save it under a new file name by selecting **File, Save As** from the pull-down menu.

User Assistance

If you need assistance with installation or if you have a damaged disk, please contact Wiley Technical Support at:

Phone:	(212) 850-6753
Fax:	(212) 850-6800 (Attention: Wiley Technical Support)
E-mail:	techhelp@wiley.com

To place additional orders or to request information about other Wiley products, please call (800) 225-5945.

Disk Contents

Exhibit 1.1	A Sample Brochure	E01.01.DOC
Exhibit 1.2	A Sample Press Release	E01.02.DOC
Exhibit 1.3	A Sample Workshop Evaluation Form	E01.03.DOC
Exhibit 2.1	Types of Seating Arrangements	E02.01.DOC
Exhibit 4.1	Presentation Outline	E04.01.DOC
Exhibit 4.2	Presentation Script	E04.02.DOC
Handout 4.1	The Nine Tasks of a Successful Marriage	H04.01.DOC
Handout 4.2	Why Marriages Succeed or Fail	H04.02.DOC
Handout 4.3	Four Skills to Build Your Marriage	H04.03.DOC
Handout 4.4	Four Marriage Destroyers	H04.04.DOC
Handout 4.5	What Do You Value?	H04.05.DOC
Handout 4.6	My Expectations	H04.06.DOC
Handout 4.7	Whose Responsibility Is It?	H04.07.DOC
Handout 4.8	What's Next?	H04.08.DOC
Exhibit 5.1	Presentation Outline	E05.01.DOC
Exhibit 5.2	Presentation Script	E05.02.DOC
Handout 5.1	12 Roadblocks to Effective Communication	H05.01.DOC
Handout 5.2	Active Listening Practice Exercises	H05.02.DOC

Handout 5.3	Listening Skills	H05.03.DOC
Handout 5.4	Assertive Communication	H05.04.DOC
Handout 5.5	You-Messages, I-Messages	H05.05.DOC
Handout 5.6	Managing Conflict	H05.06.DOC
Handout 5.7	A Better Response	H05.07.DOC
Handout 5.8	Five Ways to Interrupt Anger	H05.08.DOC
Handout 5.9	Business Skills/Marriage Skills	H05.09.DOC
Handout 5.10	What's Next?	H05.10.DOC
Exhibit 6.1	Presentation Outline	E06.01.DOC
Exhibit 6.2	Presentation Script	E06.02.DOC
Handout 6.1	The Marriage Checkup	H06.01.DOC
Exhibit 7.1	Presentation Outline	E07.01.DOC
Exhibit 7.2	Presentation Script	E07.02.DOC
Handout 7.1	Reasons for Infidelity	H07.01.DOC
Handout 7.2	Signs of Infidelity	H07.02.DOC
Handout 7.3	Infidelity Facts	H07.03.DOC
Handout 7.4	Infidelity: The Emotional Impact and Other Consequences	H07.04.DOC
Handout 7.5	How to Recover from Infidelity	H07.05.DOC
Handout 7.6	How to Prevent Infidelity	H07.06.DOC
Exhibit 8.1	Presentation Outline	E08.01.DOC
Exhibit 8.2	Presentation Script	E08.02.DOC
Handout 8.1	10 Ways to Speed Your Recovery Process	H08.01.DOC
Handout 8.2	Listening Skills	H08.02.DOC
Handout 8.3	28 Single-Parent Survival Strategies	H08.03.DOC
Exhibit 9.1	Presentation Outline	E09.01.DOC
Exhibit 9.2	Presentation Script	E09.02.DOC
Handout 9.1	Children's Divorce Rights	H09.01.DOC
Handout 9.2	36 Divorce Survival Strategies	H09.02.DOC
Exhibit 10.1	Presentation Outline	E10.01.DOC
Exhibit 10.2	Presentation Script	E10.02.DOC
Handout 10.1	12 Survival Strategies for Teens	H10.01.DOC
Handout 10.2	Who Am I?	H10.02.DOC
Handout 10.3	Assertive Behavior	H10.03.DOC
Handout 10.4	Your Opinion Counts	H10.04.DOC
Handout 10.5	Managing Your Emotions	H10.05.DOC
Exhibit 11.1	Presentation Outline	E11.01.DOC
Exhibit 11.2	Presentation Script	E11.02.DOC
Handout 11.1	Handling Conflicts	H11.01.DOC
Handout 11.2	Active Listening	H11.02.DOC
Handout 11.3	Assertive Communication Skills	H11.03.DOC
Handout 11.4	Conflict Deescalation	H11.04.DOC
Handout 11.5	Preventing Conflict	H11.05.DOC
Exhibit 12.1	Presentation Outline	E12.01.DOC
Exhibit 12.2	Presentation Script	E12.02.DOC
Handout 12.1	Facts about Caregiving	H12.01.DOC
Handout 12.2	The Five Stages of Grief Recovery	H12.02.DOC
Handout 12.3	Sources of Stress	H12.03.DOC

Handout 12.4	Signs That a Caregiver Needs Help	H12.04.DOC
Handout 12.5	Caregiver Survival Tips	H12.05.DOC
Handout 12.6	Caregiver Bill of Rights	H12.06.DOC
Exhibit 13.1	Presentation Outline	E13.01.DOC
Exhibit 13.2	Presentation Script	E13.02.DOC
Handout 13.1	Stages of Development	H13.01.DOC
Handout 13.2	How to Maintain Communication with Your Teen	H13.02.DOC
Handout 13.3	Preventing High-Risk Behavior	H13.03.DOC
Handout 13.4	Characteristics of Effective Families	H13.04.DOC
Handout 13.5	Drugs and Alcohol	H13.05.DOC
Handout 13.6	Sexuality	H13.06.DOC
Handout 13.7	Depression	H13.07.DOC
Handout 13.8	Eating Disorders	H13.08.DOC
Handout 13.9	How to Build Your Teen's Self-Esteem	H13.09.DOC

For information about the disk see the "About the Disk" section on page D.1.